THOSE DAMNED IMMIGRANTS

Those Damned Immigrants

America's Hysteria over Undocumented Immigration

Ediberto Román

With a foreword by Michael A. Olivas

NEW YORK UNIVERSITY PRESS

New York and London

NEW YORK UNIVERSITY PRESS
New York and London
www.nyupress.org

© 2013 by New York University
All rights reserved

References to Internet websites (URLs) were accurate at the time of writing.
Neither the author nor New York University Press is responsible for URLs that
may have expired or changed since the manuscript was prepared.

LIBRARY OF CONGRESS CATALOGING-IN-PUBLICATION DATA
Román, Ediberto.
Those damned immigrants: America's hysteria over undocumented immigration /
Ediberto Román; with a foreword by Michael A. Olivas.
pages cm. — (Citizenship and migration in the Americas)
Includes bibliographical references and index.
ISBN 978-0-8147-7657-5 (hardback)
1. United States—Emigration and immigration—Government policy.
2. Immigrants—United States. 3. Citizenship—United States. I. Title.
JV6483.R66   2013
364.1'370973—dc23   2013015229

New York University Press books are printed on acid-free paper, and their binding materials
are chosen for strength and durability. We strive to use environmentally responsible
suppliers and materials to the greatest extent possible in publishing our books.
Manufactured in the United States of America

10 9 8 7 6 5 4 3 2 1

For
Isabella (a.k.a Bella) Soleil Román
Your wondrous eyes and four-tooth smile light up my
world and melt me
&
Felipe Sousa Matos, Juan Jaime Rodriguez, Carlos
Alberto Roa Jr., and Maria Gabriela "Gaby" Pacheco,
a.k.a. the DREAM Walkers
Your tireless struggle for justice has inspired these efforts
&
Professor Derrick A. Bell Jr.
Your iconic work "The Space Traders" ensured I would
become a social justice scholar

CONTENTS

Ediberto Román's *Those Damned Immigrants* is a classic in the growing literature on the vast right-wing conspiracy, including the many exploitative features of capitalism in the postmodern age that attract and depend upon contingent and undocumented immigrant labor, largely from third world nations, especially the proximate Mexico, with liminal workers so desperate that they will risk life and ruin to come to *el norte*, even knowing the illegality and structural economic violence they will encounter for scandalous wages (and all too often the criminal violence they will encounter in routine hate crimes). Then, instead of rewarding them with gratitude for doing the work we do not want to do and allowing our economy to restructure at their expense, we turn around and despise them and often harm them because they are not us. And in the cruel discourse that marginalizes them as bearing "anchor babies," being "illegals," and possessing other undesirable traits—or worse, coveting our daughters—we demonize and scapegoat them. Watching these stories in the public discourse can be a sobering and largely horrific train wreck, but one that happens with much more frequency. Even the *New York Times*, largely sympathetic to immigrants, contributes to this marginalizing discursive habit by requiring its reporters to employ the term "illegal immigrant," its *New York Times Manual of Style and Usage* ensuring that the terminology is widely repeated and giving veiled support to nativists and restrictionists.

Because there is so much anti-Mexican animus evident in the quotidian public polity, especially with the escalating drug violence along the border and interior, fuelled by this country's prodigious drug appetite, it is easy to become thick-skinned about the various depictions, whether they are of the Mexicans-are-lazy-and-have-bad-cultural-traits Samuel Huntington strain or the polar opposite: they are willing to work hard for low wages and steal American jobs. But to read the extraordinary examples provided in this book is to see why the tropes have become so difficult to rebut or counter. Even worse than the scapegoating, however, is the real racial violence evident in the Marcelo Lucero case, where "beaner-hopping" thugs in Long Island killed an Ecuadorian permanent resident because they thought he was a Mexican out of status, in other words, because they thought he was "illegal," to use the all-too-common demonizing marker. Professor Román handles this example with grace and dignity, an admirable trait that I confess I have long abandoned on this subject. This cool handling of such a hot subject also shows in his review of the surprising literature on immigration, nativism, and related subjects.

He has catalogued literally dozens of such studies, and we should all be grateful for his having done so. I had seen and read many of these, but he has an encyclopedic reach and a nice synthetic touch in summarizing the complex and often contradictory findings. In fact, his singular contribution is that this work will be a starting point for any current assessment of the various strains of nativism—whether it is the failure of the DREAM which has been demogogued to death in Congress, the surprising amount of border violence that still does not satisfy the vague metrics of policy makers who insist they will not compromise on comprehensive immigration reform until the border is sealed (who knew that Democrats would be so good at border apprehensions and security and that they would remove 400,000 persons each year), or the college tuition issue in Florida and New Jersey, where citizen children are denied resident tuition (in Florida) and financial aid (in New Jersey) because their parents are undocumented. In other words, these currents and the undertow of nativism have real consequences in the lives of the undocumented and of citizens.

As Professor Román outlines with seething detail, the disembodied rule of law is employed to enact state and local ordinances to deny these workers basic benefits, safety nets, or, in Arizona and Arizona-on-steroids-Alabama, to seek out their children for school inventories, and to make it impossible for them to work in safe conditions or to walk while looking Mexican. He has helped us all by charting how both God and the devil are in the various policy details. In his damning indictment of the actual rules of the game, Professor Román is today's Edward R. Murrow, and *Those Damned Immigrants* is today's *Harvest of Shame*. His stunning book is a crash course on this important subject, and it will become a crucial tool for the accommodationist good guys if we are ever to work our way to serious structural immigration reform.

Michael A. Olivas
William B. Bates Distinguished Chair in Law,
University of Houston Law Center
Author of *No Undocumented Child Left Behind*
(New York University Press, 2012)

ACKNOWLEDGMENTS

In my previous works, I wrote the acknowledgments section after I had largely completed the manuscripts. However, in this instance I decided to write the acknowledgements before I finished the book. The reason for this approach is that I am using this section as a motivational tool to finish this labor of love.

In many respects, the motivation for this book is an unnamed child, who because of life chances, luck, or providence was born in another land to parents who crossed the "frontera" and who, for now, is part of our permanent underclass. Though a similar child born in California of undocumented parents may be a U.S. citizen in the strictest sense of the word, his or her very status is also now under attack. How is the child who recently arrived with his or her hardworking parents that much different from me, growing up in New York City's Spanish Harlem of parents born in Puerto Rico? I spoke the same language at home as these children, and we likely have many of the same cultural and religious beliefs. I am unquestionably a U.S. citizen because in 1898 the United States invaded Cuba and Puerto Rico, and soon thereafter became an empire. Just because of historical happenstance, am I more deserving of being a U.S. citizen than those children called "illegal"—part of a criminal family living as the invisible members of this society just because of parents who have crossed that imaginary dividing line known as the border?

I write for the little girl who is on my profile picture on Facebook. You see, much like the children mentioned above, the little girl pictured on my Facebook profile happened to be one of many individuals who attended a teach-in where high school and undergraduate student activists and I held a session of what is known as DREAM University at the Florida Senate building with the purpose of challenging an Arizona-like bill proposed in the Florida Senate in 2010. The little girl in my Facebook photo, who for me happens to represent every immigrant child, was about the same age as my one-year-old Bella. That little girl, whom I may never meet again, is I believe the daughter of farm workers who traveled across the state of Florida overnight on a bus to protest anti-immigrant measures. These courageous college students and farmhands risked being arrested, and many probably deported, but they nevertheless believed in the promise of this beautiful country and were willing to risk everything they knew in order to stand up for justice and respect. I was—and continue to be—in awe of them, and the beautiful little girl who is the muse for this and other of my writings moves me so much that it brings me almost to tears every time I think of and write about their efforts. I remain honored to spend time with many like them, and often see many like them at protests, rallies, teach-ins, and other related efforts. Some of the older and honorable immigrant farmers and their children often appear at events, yet they rarely speak; they just stand nearby to show their solidarity. They stand with peasant farmer nobility that reminds me of my own grandfather, and their efforts repeatedly confirm that I undertake a righteous cause. It is for these individuals, all too often voiceless, that I write, and I attempt to address issues in a fashion that may one day inspire others to know there are those of us fighting for their rights. As part of that effort, I have tried to write something here that moves beyond traditional labels and expected positions. I have attempted to write in an informed and honest way that looks beyond party lines and political expectations.

Indeed, if I do my job correctly here, I will annoy Democrats and Republicans alike. I will attack xenophobes, but I will also challenge the silent and passive so-called liberals and even the so-called radical progressives in the legal academy (and perhaps even have their ivory towers sway just a little bit). In the end, I hope to come up with solutions that, while appearing impossible, will be one of the few reputable ways to address our so-called immigration crisis.

Another source of inspiration for writing this book came from attending a symposium at Florida International University organized by the students of the FIU Public Health Immigrant Advocacy Coalition a couple of years ago. Though in the midst of a writer's block, I almost found an excuse for not attending this event; I decided to attend after learning that my friend Nilda Pedrosa, the law school's then assistant dean for development, was attending. I wanted to support all concerned, so I somewhat begrudgingly agreed. It was a fateful decision.

The event was epiphanic. During a Friday fall evening on a college campus, where I believed only a music group could attract students at that time, I noticed that well over a hundred students had come. These students were present to attend an event that was more important to them than doing what typical young adults do on a typical weekend night. I was instantly impressed with the maturity of both the organizers, who were also young, and the other attendees, the academics and activists who spoke to the group. At one point I heard the name of one of the activist groups: the DREAM Walkers. I feigned knowledge of the group, but in reality I knew nothing about them. After a talk that provided an analytical framework of the issues related to the DREAM Act, I felt a sermon-like impassioned call to action. The DREAM Walkers are a handful of undocumented activist college students who, instead of hiding in the shadows like many others subject to the fear of deportation, spoke out visibly against laws aimed at preventing them from seeking a college education. Like something right out of the civil rights movement, these youths marched 1,500 miles from Miami, Florida, to Washington, DC. I was moved almost to tears upon learning of these efforts, and I knew I needed to do what I could to help these young heroes who apparently had few traditional spokespersons. Indeed, during one of the talks, I felt what perhaps those who do not follow a religious path would find ignorant or even silly—I found a moment of almost spiritual clarity. For a good part of my adult life, I worked with almost a religious fervor to use my work to make a difference in the lives of others, but I also longed for personal recognition. I had long written about civil rights and lectured on racial justice, but I always felt I could do more for others. I sat in the auditorium that evening and decided I needed to put my many writing and speaking obligations in their proper perspective. I decided to focus on different forms of engagement and activism for immigrants' rights in general and young immigrants fighting for the right to be educated, in particular. I proudly say I dedicated this book, in addition to the joy of my life—my newborn daughter—to the four courageous souls who are the DREAM Walkers. While I hope to tell their story in a future book, I am proud to consider them my friends, souls who inspire me, and individuals I hope my own children grow to resemble.

In some way I always knew my path would cross with the DREAM Walkers. I often remember one day when I was roughly twelve years old. As I sat in front of the television in the living room of my parents' apartment, I told my sister I wanted so badly to do something important one day to help others. What exactly, I did not then know. But with a passion that I could not fully comprehend at that age, or even this age for that matter, I actually had tears in my eyes. I remember telling my sister I was so driven that it physically hurt. Almost forty years later, in a university auditorium where I knew no one, listening to these courageous young heroes who happen to be immigrant advocates, I decided that I had to use all my energies to help them. It was almost, or perhaps actually was, a religious moment where I knew I had to reenergize myself to continue to fight for those without voices. What is particularly funny and what few people know is that I am terrified of public speaking, often using notes as a means to soothe my anxiety about speaking in front of learned professionals. Interestingly, after I began to address issues of immigration in public forums, on both television and radio, many began to tell me how inspired they were to hear my voice—a voice once terrified to speak.

I also want to give a special thanks to a courageous soul whom I met only in passing, but who inspired me to have the confidence to write for others and to honestly believe I had the skill to do so—Professor Derrick A. Bell Jr. I met Professor Bell at a People of Color Conference in San Juan, Puerto Rico, just over a decade ago, and to this day I remember how thrilled I was to be sitting next to a civil rights warrior who lived his beliefs. I was also equally in awe of his humility and generosity. As many in the academy know, Professor Bell left his prestigious post at Harvard Law School because of that institution's failure to embrace diversity on its faculty.

This is an issue dear to me, as my own writings have condemned the legal academy and its so-called liberal faculties for their shameful failure at implementing diversity, especially with respect to Latino and Latina faculty and administrative leadership. These so-called forward-thinking intellectuals make allegedly bold pronouncements advocating inclusion, yet they are content to be employed by institutions as diverse as 1960s northern liberal dinner parties once were; by that I mean, it was fairly well known that during the 1960s the so-called liberal northerners were known to have gatherings where they would invite an African American guest, and a second one to demonstrate just how enlightened the hosts were in terms of diversity. Sadly, today, many law schools could not even meet that 1960s benchmark; over half of them do not have a single Latino or Latina on their tenure-track faculty. These so-called great faculties nonetheless have the power and the ability to truly commit to diversity and have their faculties resemble the population virtually overnight; ironically, such a move would stimulate this profession and ensure that a new breed of scholars would walk our hallowed halls— ah, another forthcoming book by this pugnacious author.

Indeed, when I think of Professor Bell, I realize that few in the academy have such courage and conviction, though many of us so-called race scholars sit in our offices and claim to do something profound with our writing. Professor Bell was not only a man of conviction, he was unquestionably profound in his writing. As I often tell my own students and children, Bell's "Space Traders" article changed the way I looked at the academy and our country. I will be forever indebted to a man I barely knew, but I hope to follow his trailblazing ways and am nonetheless proud and pleased to write that I had the rare privilege of meeting and admiring such a great man. And on a related note, I am also so proud to call other courageous souls like Michael Olivas, Richard Delgado, Kevin Johnson, Gerald Torres, Steven Bender, and María Pabón

López my friends. I, of course, am indebted to colleagues, friends, and respected scholars who were kind enough to read an earlier draft of this book and provide me invaluable insight and perspective. First and foremost is Linda Greene, who gave me wonderful advice about the goal of the project. I also thank other friends and colleagues, including Hannibal Travis, Steven Bender, Victor Uribe, and Nilda Pedrosa, for their valuable input on this project.

The picture on the cover of this book shows actual signs strewn all across Interstate 5 from Los Angeles to San Diego, California. I came across these signs as I was driving to give a talk before what turned out to be several hundred law professors about some of my works regarding the lack of diversity in the legal professoriate, a subject of an upcoming book. As I was racing down the highway, regretting my decision to drive instead of taking a commuter flight (which I hate), I came across these odd signs. Upon seeing them, all I could think was, "Am I being 'punk'd'? Where's the candid camera?" The only warning signs I had ever seen cautioned drivers about deer crossings or falling rocks. I had never imagined I would see an "Illegal Immigrants Crossing" sign. The only thing the sign needed to complete the stereotype as well as the objectification was for the man leading his family to be portrayed wearing a sombrero. When I later researched these signs, I learned that they were placed in order to warn drivers of so-called illegal alien families crossing the border near Camp Pendleton military base. Peculiarly, though the number of accidents diminished dramatically after other safety measures were implemented, the signs remained on Interstate 5.

Perhaps the signs are really in place to remind others of this country's so-called immigration crises. To me, these signs are a reminder of how the United States has treated valuable workers and their families who come to this country not only to make better lives for themselves, but also to give us a better quality of life. The signs reminded me of how undocumented workers and their families are invisible parts of our collective landscape, like our deer and our mountainous rock-filled roads. Undocumented immigrants can be the focus of attacks and scorn, but when they face road hazards, we place signs on the road to warn drivers not to hit them, instead of placing guardrails or even walkways. Such safety measures would obviously be deemed to tacitly support a migration created by domestic economic interests and could not be politically condoned, as they would endorse lawless behavior.

As with most acknowledgments, I would like to thank a host of individuals who were indispensable in making this project a success. First and foremost, I would like to thank Debbie Gershenowitz, formerly New York University Press's law editor and now the history editor at Cambridge University Press. Debbie is a brilliant editor who is always accessible and consistently adds invaluable contributions to any project, and she has become an important mentor. I have never mentioned this to her, but after she telephoned me and expressed great interest in publishing this book, based largely on an article I had provided her, I for the first time truly felt like an accomplished scholar and suspected that things were going to change in terms of my profile in the academy. Needless to say, she also contributed greatly to that change by her mentorship. And I am confident that by the time this book is published a host of other significant books from some of the country's leading academics will be in the process of being published in this series. I will always be indebted to my first law editor. I also want to thank New York University Press's new law editor, Clara Platter, for her assistance and support. While we have only begun to work together on the Citizenship and Migration in America series, I have no doubt we will continue to make the series not only the academy's leading immigration law series, but also the leading law series in general. I also want to thank my home institution, Florida International University College of Law, and my new dean, Alex Acosta. While the last few years at a new and growing institution have had their share of disappointments and challenges, it is refreshing to be at an institution that is led by a fair and honorable person. I also want to thank FIU's president, Mark Rosenberg, for supporting all Miami area students, including its immigrant students. Indeed, just a short time before this book went to press, I learned that FIU is the first public university in the state to provide out-of-state tuition waivers to deferred action recipients. So proud of my home institution! I often remember the wise advice President Rosenberg gave me several years ago: "Do the right thing and do it the right way." The challenging task undertaken here, which I have often thought should have been written by an entire governmental agency, think tank, or institute, I trust is an example of both doing the right thing and doing it the right way.

I also want to thank my many fellow travelers who have always added to engagement and dialogue. While the list of leading lights is too long to complete here, some are worth noting: Stephen H. Legomsky, Gerald Neuman, Gerald Torres, Peter Spiro, Stanley Fish, Angela Onwuachi-Willig, and Victor Romero. A special thank you is in order to my mentor, at times harshest critic, and author of the foreword to this book, Michael Olivas. Without his tireless work over several decades to diversify the legal academy, I know I would not have become a law professor. I feel blessed that his efforts did not end when I entered the academy. He has always been there to provide me with tough but wise advice. I guess my students, both former and current, should know that Professor Olivas is my Professor Román.

I am also indebted to FIU College of Law Librarian Marisol Floren for her amazing assistance with research. I so appreciate that she regularly listens to her voicemail, where I am sure she has heard my many late-night requests for sometimes obscure studies and reports. I, of course, want to thank my research assistant, Jarred Reiling. I expect him to continue to work tirelessly on this and other projects. I cannot wait until we write a book on other issues relating to equality, including the equal marriage debate. Jarred's talent, honor, and poise have always impressed me. He is a truly amazing attorney, and now copyeditor, but perhaps most important, an even more impressive person. I am so proud to have worked with him, and to consider him a friend. I must also thank my graduate assistant Casey King for all his efforts with this project. I am indebted to Steven Chambers, Ben Crego and Rebecca Roque for their incredible efforts with proofing this manuscript and checking every footnote, often with very tough time constraints. I want to thank Lisbeth D'Lima, an amazing assistant and great proofreader. Her efforts, though surprising at first, now never stop impressing me. Much appreciation is also sent to every student I have had the great honor to teach. While I am certain that some may not have appreciated my demanding ways, and some may have a fair amount of dislike for me because of their grades, the truth is I have always been so honored and proud to teach them, and always wanted the very best for them in their professional development.

On the personal side, I want to express first my appreciation and love for my children, Katerina, Christian, Nicholas, Andres, and Isabella, a.k.a. Bella. You are my blessings, and I thank the good Lord every day for having you as part of my life. As a sappy dad, I often go on and on about my children in my other books, and I want to leave a special note for my beautiful, brilliant, and powerful Bella. While you may be but a bit over a year old, I want to let you know that Daddy loves you more than a bear loves honey. Your smiling eyes melt my heart and your smile is the most beautiful thing I have ever seen. I cherish every moment I get to spend with you (P.S. Mom thinks I am crazy about you because you look like her—as you would say, "Silly!"). Though you are barely talking at the age of one, I know that, much like your siblings, you are brilliant, but sadly for them, you are probably the brightest of the bunch. You are my sunshine, and I thank the Lord every day for bringing you and the rest of the gang into my life. While your world will hopefully be very different from the one I grew up in, I want you to remember that your gender and your ethnicity will be assets that will provide you the strength to overcome any challenge you face in life. I had also better mention my other kiddos. Kati: you are the family's lighthouse—when we are lost at sea, your beauty, wisdom, and kindness lead us to you. Christian: you are growing to be such an impressive young man: smart, athletic, kind, and of course, handsome. I hope you continue to work on your martial arts studies; you have a rare talent, but are never to beat Dad. Nick: you are my brave little man; Daddy wishes you would never have any pains in life, and I pray you will be better soon. AJ: you adore Mommy more than Dad, your wisdom thus leaves room for growth, but in all honesty, you and Nick are the bravest little men I know. Your doctors said your eyes would give you trouble and you could not play the sport you love—baseball—but you have proven them wrong (i.e., as I proofread the book on a Saturday morning at the baseball field, you hit another double with our magic bat—perhaps another little sign?). You see, AJ, tenacity is a family and cultural trait. Last but never least, I want to thank my beautiful wife for always supporting my efforts and encouraging me even when I was at times uncertain whether my scholarship would hurt my career. She always correctly reminded me that I did not write for personal advancement, because if such was my goal, I would have continued to address far less controversial areas, such as securities law. As always, she has provided me with profound wisdom. I remain thankful for my primary blessings and will always love all of you guys!

1

Introduction

"Ladies and gentlemen, we interrupt our program . . . to bring you a special bulletin." From the depths of your nightmares comes an untold terror.
From across your borders come "cool and unsympathetic" beings who
gaze on this land "with envious eyes, . . . slowly and surely dr[awing] their
plans against [you]." A faint warning glistens across the wire as the terror grows. "Ladies and gentlemen, this is the most terrifying thing I have
ever witnessed. . . . Wait a minute! Someone's crawling out. . . . Someone
or . . . something. . . . Good heavens, something's wriggling out of the
shadows like a [brown] snake. Now it's another one, and another." The
massed crowds focus intensely as the being's face rises from the darkness.
"It's indescribable. I can hardly force myself to keep looking at it." As you
move closer and closer, the being is "raising up." Finally one being comes
into focus; you see what horror lies in front of you. Confusion reigns
supreme as the masses try to make sense of what has occurred before
their very eyes. Then, the soothing voice of the government streams from
the airwaves to help them make sense of what is happening:

"Citizens of the nation: I shall not try to conceal the gravity of the situation that confronts the country, nor the concern of the government in

protecting the lives and property of its people. However, I wish to impress upon you—private citizens and public officials, all of you—the urgent need of calm and resourceful action. Fortunately, this formidable enemy is still confined to a comparatively small area, and we may place our faith in the military forces to keep them there. In the meantime placing our faith in God we must continue the performance of our duties, each and every one of us, so that we may confront this destructive adversary with a nation united, courageous, and consecrated to the preservation of human supremacy on this earth. I thank you." Your mind races in a futile attempt to make sense of what has occurred. "All that happened before the arrival of these monstrous creatures in the world now seems part of another life, . . . a life that has no continuity with the present." Finally, the realization strikes you: "They [are] wreck[ing] the greatest country in the world." They're nothing like you—they need to be stopped. . . .[1]

It does not take a stretch of the imagination to see how the above narrative (using direct quotes from the infamous 1938 *War of the Worlds* broadcast) could easily be tomorrow's leading news bulletin concerning this country's alleged immigration crisis.[2] Following increased domestic oversight and arguably isolationist sentiments after September 11, 2001, media,[3] political,[4] academic,[5] and would-be academic[6] figures have effectively caused a furor, almost to the point of panic, over the issue,[7] using virulent attacks aimed largely against the Latino and Latina immigrant groups crossing the Mexican border.[8] FBI reports on domestic hate crimes after 2001, for instance, indicate that such crimes against Latinos and Latinas surged from 2003 to 2006.[9] The Mexican American Legal Defense and Educational Fund (MALDEF) blames anti-immigrant sentiments for the surge.[10] Surprisingly, the verbal assaults on the immigrant community, which are often bigoted and thus shameful,[11] have thus far gone largely unaddressed in public opinion circles, in part because the alleged basis for limiting immigration is often couched in vague language of "national security" and "the war on terror."[12] While some view the concerns as mudslinging aimed at stirring racist and xenophobic fears,[13] sadly many Americans have accepted and expressed agreement with the anti-immigrant attacks.[14]

Several questions arise from tales like the one above—as well as the tales heard virtually every day from the media, including from figures like Lou Dobbs and Bill O'Reilly: are these all-too-often unseemly accounts and tales of woe accurate? Or is it that this country has abandoned the noble ethos of inclusion that is engrained in the spirit of our laws?

On the one hand, this country demonstrates an inclusive and welcoming ethos, iconically engraved on the tablet of Lady Liberty. Yet, repeatedly throughout this country's history, there have been less than proud moments of hate targeted against the immigrant community.[15] In a land that is self-proclaimed as a land of immigrants, there exists a history of slavery against Africans, attempted genocide against its indigenous peoples, and anti-immigrant efforts such as the Alien and Sedition Act of 1798, Operation Wetback of the 1950s, race-based immigration quotas, and denials of equal rights based upon sexual orientation.[16] Noble notions of sanctuary have often brushed up against fear and hatred of the "other." This tension is witnessed not only in legal moments but also in consequential statements of who we are as a people, in both our proclamations and our literature.

Compare, for instance, the inspirational statement of America's inclusive credo, perhaps also our immigration mantra, in Emma Lazarus's 1883 poem "New Colossus":

> Not like the brazen giant of Greek fame,
> With conquering limbs astride from land to land;
> Here at our sea-washed, sunset gates shall stand
> A mighty woman with a torch, whose flame
> Is the imprisoned lightning, and her name
> Mother of Exiles. From her beacon-hand
> Glows world-wide welcome; her mild eyes command
> The air-bridged harbor that twin cities frame.
> "Keep ancient lands, your storied pomp!" cries she

> With silent lips. "Give me your tired, your poor,
> Your huddled masses yearning to breathe free,
> The wretched refuse of your teeming shore.
> Send these, the homeless, tempest-tossed to me,
> I lift my lamp beside the golden door!"[17]

These welcoming words are in stark contrast with the sentiments of others, both during Lazarus's period and during recent xenophobic moments. For instance, Thomas Bailey Aldrich's 1895 poem "Unguarded Gates" offers a very different vision of how we should view ourselves and immigrants:

> Wide open and unguarded stand our gates,
> And through them presses a wild motley throng—
> Men from the Volga and the Tartar steppes,
> Featureless figures of the Hoang-Ho,
> Malayan, Scythian, Teuton, Kelt, and Slav,
> Flying the Old World's poverty and scorn;
> These bringing with them unknown gods and rites,
> Those, tiger passions, here to stretch their claws.
> In street and alley what strange tongues are loud,
> Accents of menace alien to our air,
> Voices that once the Tower of Babel knew!
> O Liberty, white Goddess! Is it well
> To leave the gates unguarded? On thy breast
> Fold Sorrow's children.[18]

Slightly more than a century later, a similarly unkind picture of immigrants occurred in a ditty that made its way around the Internet:

> I come for visit, get treated regal,
> So I stay, who care I illegal?
> Cross border, poor & broke,
> Take bus, see Customs bloke.

Nice man treats me good in there,
Say I need to see welfare.
Welfare say "You come no more,
We send cash right to your door."
Welfare checks, they make you wealthy,
Medi-cal, it keep you healthy!
By & by, I got plenty money,
Thanks, American working dummy.
Write to friends in motherland,
Tell them come as fast as you can.
They come in rags & Chubby trucks,
I buy big house with welfare bucks.
They all come, we live together
To live off America and make life better!
Fourteen families now move in,
Neighbor's patience growing thin.
Finally white boy moves away,
I buy house and then I say,
"Find more aliens," house I rent,
In the garden I put a tent.
Send for family (they just trash)
But they draw more welfare cash!
Everything is mucho good,
Soon we own the neighborhood.
We have hobby, it's called breeding,
Welfare pay for baby feeding.
Kids need dentist? Wife needs pills,
We get free, we have no bills.
American crazy, he pay all year
To keep his Welfare running here.
We think America damn good place!
Too damn good for white man race.
If they no like us, they can go,
Got lots of room in Mexico.[19]

Today public opinion on immigration seems to have shifted to the side of the anti-immigrant advocates.[20] Anti-immigrant attitudes are widely disseminated in political circles, on talk radio, and in countless television depictions. Indeed, it appears one cannot go a week listening to talk radio hosts like Rush Limbaugh or watching cable television stations like Fox News or CNN without witnessing offensive statements concerning undocumented immigrants.

Politicians also take advantage of the defenseless and make similar comments in order to appear tough on crime and national security. These now-common attacks against immigrants, particularly undocumented immigrants, are not unlike criticisms against virtually any other minority group in this land at one point or another in this country's history. As will be demonstrated in the pages to come, much of the anti-immigrant attacks are so utterly racist and offensive that one would think they would not be tolerated. As witnessed by the condemnation of the talk show host Don Imus for his shameful attack against the Rutgers women's basketball team, our society tends to have little tolerance for openly racist diatribes, yet such diatribes are regularly launched against undocumented immigrants. Could it be because this group is considered "illegal" and therefore deserving of any criticism, no matter how unfair? Such a poor excuse to spew hate and intolerance needs to be challenged and ended. This book undertakes that noble but daunting task.

The hateful rhetoric often associated with undocumented immigrants, more commonly known as illegal immigrants,[21] has virtually silenced those in favor of rational proposals for reform. Factually flawed and baseless anti-immigrant venom, often spewed unchecked, is what this book aspires to be the antidote for. While logic, decency, and humanity could be the sole basis to challenge contemporary vitriolic attacks against undocumented immigrants, attempts are made here to undertake what has yet to be undertaken—to engage in an informed and factually based retort to the unfounded speculations, assumptions, and attacks made against undocumented immigrants. The current popular rhetoric positions the status of immigrant as a "social identity

[that] has been plagued by the mark of illegality, which in much public discourse means that they are criminals and thus illegitimate members of society undeserving of social benefits, including citizenship."[22] While the pro-immigrant effort is much needed, given the lack of informed engagement, it is not an easy one. In part because studies addressing the cultural and economic consequences of immigration are numerous and often driven by a variety of interest groups, providing an informed analysis is challenging, to say the least.

Policy makers will hopefully be informed by this in-depth analysis of the leading credible studies on what is one of the most contentious, yet important, public policy debates of this generation. Another important goal here is to identify the legal consequences of basing public policy on factually flawed reports or, worse yet, baseless anti-immigrant rhetoric.

As a final step, an economically sound and humane proposal for change will be made. Among other things, this proposal will stress the need to end the obfuscating and unsound rhetoric associated with the value of undocumented immigrants. It will also address the concern of the national government as well as state and local communities concerning the costs and fears associated with immigration. The free rider problem associated with domestic business sectors that actually create the demand for undocumented immigration will also be confronted. In particular, the domestic business sectors that create the demand for immigration without being responsible for the consequences will be asked to take up their respective obligations to our society.

Finally, this project will propose comprehensive immigration reform that will illustrate how to address three important groups of immigrants: (1) young adults seeking to attain a college education but often denied because of their "illegal" status as a result of their "crossing the border" as children with their parents (who were themselves seeking employment), (2) the rest of the approximately eleven million other undocumented immigrants residing and working in this country, and (3) all future immigrants seeking to work in this country.

Those on either side of the national and state immigration debate as well as leaders all along the political spectrum may very well become or even angered by both the examination undertaken here and ⟩ns proposed. The reason for this prediction is that this project ⸳⸳⸳ uⁿuertaken to merely point fingers. Rather, a primary goal here is to address the fact that with issues as controversial yet important as immigration—which touches upon a host of other issues, including the economy, national security, and foreign relations—the differing sides tend not to address each other. In the end, everyone tends to preach to the converted on their respective side of the issue. Apparently, each side hopes that if they repeat themselves long enough, they will attract more followers. That is not the goal here.

What will be undertaken in the forthcoming pages is more than merely engaging in retelling tales of woe. In terms of an overview of what is forthcoming, and perhaps at the risk of oversimplifying this herculean endeavor, this project aims to undertake and achieve what no single work has yet accomplished. It attempts, in one document, to first identify the leading attacks against undocumented immigrants; then, using empirical data, it will examine the validity of those attacks, demonstrating how such attacks are far from new in this country's history; subsequently, it will establish how such attacks have shaped policy in the past and will likely shape policy in the future unless exposed. Finally, this project will propose a means to resolve the current immigration stalemate.

This introductory chapter provides a brief overview of the entire project and its goals. In addition, this chapter will begin to explore the current debate concerning undocumented immigration, and ultimately provide the reader with the author's vision for proposed comprehensive immigration reform. Chapter 2 will examine in greater detail the dominant narrative concerning undocumented immigration, which is largely negative. The chapter will explore the leading anti-immigrant attacks in the media, by politicians, and others who claim that (1) immigrants are part of a cultural and population overthrow; (2) immigrants are part of a crime wave entering this country, and (3) immigrants are hurting our national economy by, among other things, stealing American jobs and lowering domestic wages. Chapter 3 will respond to the allegations raised in chapter 2, through the use of empirical studies from a broad selection of sources, including the federal government, leading immigrant rights advocacy groups, and conservative think tanks that have examined the validity claims raised in the first chapter. The fourth chapter will explore the troubling issues not resolved by the conclusions reached in chapter 3. Chapter 4 will explore the costs of undocumented immigration on local and state governments. In addition to exploring a problem largely unaddressed by either the federal government or advocates of immigrant rights, this chapter also examines the largely ill-advised efforts by state and local governments to address the immigration issue themselves. Chapter 5 will take a slight shift in focus and examine this country's history with respect to South American immigration, focusing on Mexican immigration. The reason for this historical focus is to demonstrate that the current anti-immigrant narratives are far from new, and the current narrative is eerily similar to attacks of the past. The chapter also demonstrates the cycle this country is in the midst of and will likely continue if it continues to demonize immigrants despite the ongoing demand for these immigrant workers. Another purpose of chapter 5 is to serve as a historical example of how past hateful rhetoric affected public policy concerning immigration, suggesting that similar attacks may very well continue to affect current and future policy. Chapter 6 examines sociological and psychological studies on the likely public policy effects of the use of hateful narratives that stereotype and stigmatize undocumented immigrants. This chapter thus serves the important function of drawing a nexus between arguable social ills—scapegoating and stereotyping—and the creation of unsound laws. Finally, chapter 7 will explore the existing varying views on how to resolve the so-called immigration crisis. Ultimately, this chapter will propose a pragmatic and economically sound solution that includes the creation of a fair and accountable guest worker program for future immigrants, adoption of a form of the DREAM Act, and procedures and priorities that address the eleven million undocumented individuals already in this country.

A primary goal of this project is to begin a movement to change immigration discourse, to replace the hateful rhetoric that dominates the current debate concerning undocumented immigration with facts based on empirical data. This project will undertake an essential but often devalued task by legal academics of exhaustively compiling the leading empirical studies to address an important societal misconception. In this case, the studies will disprove what has thus far been repeatedly argued but not proven, namely, (1) that undocumented immigration creates a cultural and population threat, (2) that undocumented immigration is causing a crime wave in this country, and (3) that undocumented immigrants are harmful to the U.S. economy and domestic workers.

Many studies addressing these issues lead to conclusions that some may view as pro-immigrant, but that is because the data support such conclusions. This project will nonetheless not merely take a side and repeat old positions. It will address questions that both sides have thus far failed to contend with. The two sides in the current immigration debate bring to mind the hackneyed phrase "ships passing in the night," with the political left arguing in favor of a human rights–focused agenda and stressing the positive impact undocumented immigrants provide our national economy, and the more responsible anti-immigrant political right raising alarms over national security and the negative consequences of undocumented immigration on state and local economies.

In reality, both groups' positions have merit, yet until now, few have tried to confront the opposing views and their relative strengths and weaknesses. Before engaging in such an examination, this project will dispel the all-too-common illegitimate rhetoric associated with undocumented immigration. In addition, the economic and cultural realities of undocumented immigration will be addressed in order to trace our long history of conflicted attitudes toward immigration. The goal is to document how today's rhetoric is almost identical to that of the past, and it is those old tales that have helped shape current views as well as ill-advised national and local policies. Thus, the purpose of this historical effort is to highlight the need to engage in fact-based, historically informed discussions that may lead to sound policy in order to avoid repeating unseemly episodes from our past, such as Operation Wetback and other shameful events.

I will examine studies from the social sciences such as sociology and psychology in order to draw a nexus between the current stigmatizing narratives concerning undocumented immigrants and the legal consequences of such stigmatizing and stereotyping efforts—namely, creation of unsound policy decisions influenced by public discourse. Thus, the very use of the hateful anecdotes that characterize the current state of immigration discourse addressed in the next chapter will lay the groundwork for the penultimate chapter, which will draw a nexus between hateful speech and its ability to affect views and perceptions and consequently affect policy decisions, and thus immigration law. Looking to the role of stigma and stereotyping in creating "the other," and how such phenomena actually help foster hatred and skewed policy decisions on immigration, I will examine a number of psychological and sociological studies on theories such as transference, dissonance, and other phenomena. How this country has allowed for rhetoric filled with ignorance and even bias to frame not only how we think of immigrants, but also how we think of all Hispanics and other perceived immigrant groups, will be explored in order to examine how this country creates policies and laws that often harm the country's own economic interests as well as the interests of important sectors of society, such as the agriculture and construction industries. In the process of this examination, the role of the all-too-often missing party in the immigration debate— the domestic business sectors that drive the demand for undocumented workers—will be explored.

Typically, in current immigration discussions, pundits and politicians alike condemn undocumented immigrants in large part because they represent an easy target—they are no one's constituents and are thus perceived to be voiceless. As a result, it is easy to blame these silent members of our society, especially when we place labels such as "illegal" on them. Yet the vast majority of undocumented immigrants do not come here to steal or take from this country; they come here to work, and they do so in response to the demand created by domestic business sectors seeking low-cost labor. Immigration, especially undocumented immigration, is thus primarily responsive, and directly correlated to domestic economic conditions. After all, as witnessed in the last decade, when the domestic economy is suffering, undocumented immigration rates decline.

In many respects, the silent parties to the debate—business sectors such as the agricultural, construction, and service industries—are themselves the economic free riders. These sectors of the economy create the demand for undocumented workers, yet they are rarely blamed for creating the demand; they are not held accountable in efforts to address immigration; and they are even less likely to speak up on undocumented immigration, despite benefitting from it. One reason for this silence is perhaps the fear of being attacked, or more likely the fear of being asked to make laws such as minimum wage laws and the Fair Labor Standards Act applicable to all individuals, including undocumented immigrants.

Obviously, such impositions of laws on important domestic business sectors may have a significant impact on these sectors' demand for undocumented immigration. The alternative to full application of the domestic employment laws to the undocumented would be compromised positions on the laws, that is, another baseline of minimum wages for guest workers in exchange for certain basic benefits for the previously undocumented. For instance, in exchange for allowing domestic business to openly attract low-wage immigrant workers, employees in these areas would be offered access to employer-sponsored or -subsidized non-emergency healthcare centers. By creating such legal exceptions, a guest worker program would legally create a demand for labor that is not easily found in this country. Such a proposal would also provide some basic human rights to largely defenseless currently undocumented immigrants. In any event, a guest worker program that would also ensure that businesses protect and secure all their workers with some form of insurance has the benefit of sound economic policy to those businesses, but also adds the benefits to local communities and states that thus far have had to bear most of the burden of paying for the healthcare of undocumented immigrants within their jurisdictions.

Perhaps annoying classic critical scholars, such as critical legal studies scholars, this project will go beyond identifying significant social problems and will seek workable solutions to all legitimate sides in the debate. The political right, often associated with anti-immigrant stances, must contend with the fact that much of the popular rhetoric associated with immigration is based on faulty information and is rife with simplistic, racially and ethnically biased, and illegitimate motivations. All sides of the debate will be held accountable and must, as a first step to real change, dispel basic misperceptions, such as the popular view that there is in fact an immigration crisis or a so-called broken immigration system. For instance, too often the media and even political leaders make assertions concerning a so-called immigration crisis in this country. Indeed, the Obama administration has repeatedly made statements to the effect that our country's immigration system is broken. For instance, in an official statement on the subject of immigration reform, the administration observed,

> The President reiterated his commitment to comprehensive immigration reform that both strengthens security at our borders while restoring accountability to *the broken immigration system*, and pointed out that *perpetuating a broken immigration system* is not an option if America is to win the future.[23]

These assertions, though made by a cabinet-level official, are not correct. Using the figure of eleven million to conclude that there is a national crisis is faulty for a number of reasons. First, that figure is often bandied about to cause a visceral reaction to the sheer number of "illegals" walking our streets. Yet empirical data from the federal government itself demonstrate that, believe it or not, the figure of eleven million is unremarkable. The White House and major media outlets never point out that eleven million is actually small relative to the total population of this country.

Simply put, when the federal government commissioned a study on the impact of undocumented immigration, the blue-ribbon team of nationally respected economists, social scientists, and demographers found that the most appropriate way to measure immigration was to look at it relative to the overall population. The panel concluded that undocumented immigration, despite the popular belief that it is almost destroying our country and way of life, is actually at one of its lowest rates in our country's history. Yet, despite this two-volume study being released over a decade ago, no mainstream voice addresses this fact, and especially not the media.

Related to the above mischaracterization is the popular belief that undocumented immigrants are a drain on our national economy and that they steal jobs from domestic workers. Once again, using a host of studies from across the political spectrum, this book conclusively lays these baseless assertions to rest. Undocumented immigrants actually are a net benefit to the national economy for a host of reasons. They actually increase wages of domestic workers, and they tend not to displace domestic workers. The two groups (undocumented immigrants and domestic workers) are simply not equivalent. Again, it needs to be stressed that unlike the widely disseminated statements that we often hear concerning undocumented immigration, the arguments made here are based in fact and empiricism. Indeed, the positions taken here come from the most respected examinations by the most respected experts.

The so-called sympathetic left, for its part, must grapple with the largely dismissed reality that undocumented immigration does have a financial impact, at least in the short term, on local and state governments. For instance, it simply defies logic to suggest that undocumented immigrants, who often do not have healthcare insurance, do not pose some added expenses in the healthcare field, when even laypeople know that undocumented immigrants as a last resort go to public hospitals when in need of medical assistance, especially when facing emergency situations. Moreover, when undocumented immigrants reside in the United States with their families, which is not that unusual, there is the added economic burden of educating undocumented children and U.S. citizen children of the undocumented. The simple fact that there are no conclusive studies to establish the above positions (because, as the federal government has found in at least two occasions, the healthcare industry does a poor job of tracking patients) does not undercut their logic concerning certain obvious costs of undocumented immigration to local economies.

After annoying perhaps all sectors of conventional wisdom, as well as both sides of the domestic political spectrum, I set forth proposed solutions with the goal of leading to change. The proposal I will make in chapter 7 ultimately recognizes the overall economic benefits of undocumented immigration, and uses that fact to address local and state concerns over immigration. This country also needs to acknowledge the certain realities of undocumented immigration. For instance, the country must realize that few domestic workers want to do the work undocumented immigrants have historically undertaken. Consequently, society must stop scapegoating important sectors of this society. In addition, the federal government needs to be prepared to address the fact that certain states and local economies bear significant burdens to their healthcare and education systems. The federal government needs to be prepared to use the overall fiscal gain of undocumented immigration to reimburse those states that bear more than their share of added costs stemming from undocumented immigration. This is actually not such a novel idea. Roughly a decade ago, several states made a similar request to the federal government, which ultimately was dismissed without much attention. Such an effort must be continued and political pressure needs to be put on the federal government. If nothing else, equity calls for such action. In the face of all this energy spent on talk radio and by political demagogues demonizing and scapegoating undocumented immigrants, a basic grassroots call for honest discussion and engagement needs to be undertaken. The centuries-long history of conflicted attitudes toward undocumented immigrants must be ended. For instance, in times of economic growth when immigrants are needed, the government institutes policies that encourage undocumented immigration or at least turn a blind eye toward it; but in times of perceived political unrest such as war or in times of economic downturn, society blames undocumented immigrants for society's economic problems. Instead of repeating this cycle, society needs to come to terms with the realities of immigration, which would include all benefits and challenges associated with all forms of immigration.

I will set forth my comprehensive reform proposal in detail in chapter 7; for now I will simply list the proposal's five main components: (1) a guest worker program with provisions for workers' rights and for federal aid to states; (2) passage of DREAM Act legislation; and (3) a set of clear and stringent requirements by which an undocumented immigrant can initiate a process toward citizenship; (4) a plan to authorize the granting of lawful permanent resident status to immigrants who have received a master's or PhD degree from an American university in the science, technology, engineering, or math (STEM) fields; and (5) a reform plan to streamline skilled worker visa programs in order to promote the best and the brightest to study in needed fields. This proposal will hopefully provide a blueprint for true change for policy makers sincerely interested in resolving the immigration debate.

2

Anti-Immigrant Rhetoric

Rhetoric is widely known as the art of discourse, but the art in the immigration context is filled with venom. Central to the modern-day immigrant rhetoric is the so-called mass invasion at our borders.[1] Not unlike the momentary hysteria associated with the *War of the Worlds* broadcast, media, politicians, and conservative pundits all too often sound alarms of an effort to take over America,[2] and of undocumented immigration's alleged horrific impact on the U.S. economy.[3] Similarly alarmist claims are made about an alleged crime wave that will inevitably result from the mass migration.[4] These claims are made with little or no evidentiary support, yet they have captured the public imagination, especially in a presidential election year.[5] Unfortunately, such calls will likely be the focus of political and public policy debates for decades to come.[6] Somewhat surprisingly, not unlike the recent eerie depiction of ugly brown figures invading New York City in the film *Cloverfield*,[7] today's invasion—of so-called illegals—is largely accepted as an inevitable future for America. Kevin Johnson describes these "metaphorical wars" as a "hijacking of the debate over immigration reform by monsters, ghosts, and goblins."[8] Johnson analyzes how these rhetorical devices obstruct attempts at substantive improvements in immigration laws, despite the pressing need for change. Similarly, the immigration scholar Michael Olivas notes that "immigration restrictionists have resorted to false stories and scapegoating in their campaign to vilify immigrants."[9] Lisa Flores acknowledges the power of rhetoric in the immigration arena, especially when stemming from media portrayals: "publics come to understand immigration and to conceive of immigrants via participation in mediated discussions. Ono and Sloop . . . make this powerful point: '[immigration] rhetoric *shifts* borders, changing what they mean publicly, influencing public policy, altering the ways borders affect people, and circumscribing political responses.'"[10] According to Leo Chavez in his provocative book *The Latino Threat*, "The Latino Threat Narrative posits that Latinos are not like previous immigrant groups, who ultimately became part of the nation. . . . [T]hey are part of an invading force from south of the border that is bent on reconquering land that was formerly theirs (the U.S. Southwest) and destroying the American way of life."[11]

The Rhetoric of the Politicos

Consider the tenor of recent attacks. For instance, Alabama state senator Scott Beason, the politician who sponsored Alabama's recent anti-immigrant legislation, HB 56, proposed in a 2011 speech that the way to solve the problem of illegal immigration was for people to "empty the clip." According to Beason, "The reality is that if you allow illegal immigration to continue in your area you will destroy yourself eventually. . . . If you don't believe illegal immigration will destroy a community go and check out parts of Alabama around Arab and Albertville."[12]

These attacks are waged not only by fairly unknown, arguably narrow-minded political hacks, but also by leading presidential candidates. For instance, during an October 2011 talk in Tennessee, Herman Cain, once the leading Republican presidential candidate, proposed creating an electrified fence that would kill all trespassers as one solution for illegal immigration:

I just got back from China. Ever heard of the Great Wall of China? It looks
pretty sturdy. And that sucker is real high. I think we can build one if we
want to! We have put a man on the moon, we can build a fence! Now, my
fence might be part Great Wall and part electrical technology. . . . It will
be a twenty foot wall, barbed wire, electrified on the top, and on this side
of the fence, I'll have that moat that President Obama talked about. And
I would put those alligators in that moat![13]

The then political frontrunner for the presidency of the United States,
Cain later explained that "America's got to learn how to take a joke."[14] But
Cain's so-called joke was welcomed with cheers of support, not laugh-
ter.[15] Cain's effort was classic pandering. As one newspaper observed,

On Saturday, surging GOP presidential contender Herman Cain twice
suggested that if elected, he wouldn't just build an anti-immigration fence
along the U.S.-Mexico border—he'd electrify it. "And there's going to be a
sign on the other side saying, 'It will kill you—Warning,'" he told a crowd
in Harriman, Tenn., to loud cheers. Cain also said he'd consider station-
ing U.S. troops "with real guns and real bullets" along the border. Asked
about his remarks on Sunday morning's *Meet the Press*, Cain said: "That's
a joke. . . . That's not a serious plan. I've also said America needs to get a
sense of humor." Should we take his "joke" seriously?

He was pandering, not joking: Conservatives always use this "it was a
joke" dodge when caught saying "something disgusting to pander to the
loony base," says Charles Johnson in *Little Green Footballs*. The only joke
here is Cain falling back on such a "tired and worn out" excuse. And even
if "Cain's little xenophobic jest about killing Mexicans" was meant to be
funny, note that his eager audience was cheering, not laughing.[16]

Sadly, as the following pages will demonstrate, such comments are
not uncommon, and all too often have no repercussions. Imagine a
political candidate, a presidential candidate no less, making a comment
to a largely white audience that we should kill all violators of any law,
fully recognizing that the violators are of one ethnic or racial group that

is not white. Such a comment being made by an African American is perhaps even more unsettling, given the well-known struggle for equality of African Americans in this land. Cain's alleged misguided humor was an effort to attack a group that would not and could not respond. In other words, Herman Cain acted like a classic coward.

Cain continued to offer apologies and insist that he was joking,[17] but his excuse, as one might expect, did not sit well with many Latinos and Latinas. A Latino Republican group called Somos Republicans sent Cain an open letter:

> In recent months, you have told audiences that as president you will build a "Great Wall of China" with an electrified fence and alligator-filled moat. One time you even compared immigrants to invading Huns. Then, as these speeches become controversial, you tried to evade criticism claiming the proposal was all just a joke. Mr. Cain, jokes involving killing people is not a suitable topic for a joke. Hundreds of migrants die crossing our Southern border each year, and as a result this is an extremely sensitive topic, especially among most of America's 51 million Hispanics. I'm sure most Americans would not appreciate jokes about 9-11, and most blacks would not appreciate jokes about hanging blacks either. Please refrain from ever repeating this proposal again.[18]

Through this rhetoric, Cain appeared to form a bandwagon that others readily joined. Soon after Cain's comments, the presidential candidate Michele Bachmann signed a pledge promising to finish the fence between the United States and Mexico, and went one step further, a double fence. "I will secure the border," she pledged.[19]

During this announcement, Bachmann followed the tried and true approach, using alleged data to support her policy. As will be demonstrated later in this book, Bachmann's position is not only unsupported by data, but flat-out wrong. As ABC News reported, "Bachmann said illegal immigration costs the country $1 billion a year and tied the flow of undocumented immigrants to the unemployment rate and national security."[20] The only way this figure comes close to being accurate is if one considers the enormously expensive but largely unsuccessful efforts at taking an "enforcement only" approach to immigration. The reason for this is, as will be demonstrated in the next chapter, that undocumented immigrants are not a drain on our national economy. Indeed, they are a net plus in terms of economic benefit to our society.

Attacks against undocumented immigrants, as in previous periods, were a central issue in the 2012 presidential election. Immigration is always an easy target for candidates seeking to appear strong on national defense and crime and perhaps even appealing to xenophobic sentiments, as in Herman Cain's comments mentioned above. Presidential candidates will likely use or allude to these issues. During the 2012 presidential primaries, the former Massachusetts governor Mitt Romney attempted to demonstrate his strength on foreign affairs as well as his conservative roots by attacking the front-runner, the former Texas governor Rick Perry, for Perry's alleged pro-immigrant history, as reported, for example, in *Politico*:

> "We must stop providing the incentives that promote illegal immigration," Romney told more than 100 people attending a Republican Hispanic conference. "As governor, I vetoed legislation that would have provided in-state tuition rates to illegal immigrants and I strengthened the authority our state troopers had to enforce existing immigration laws." . . .
>
> [I]mmigration is a new issue of focus for Romney this election cycle, and his campaign knows Perry, 61, is already facing criticism from conservatives for not taking a hard-enough line.
>
> For instance, in 2001 Perry signed a version of the "DREAM Act" that made Texas the first state to allow in-state tuition to undocumented immigrants—much like the bill Romney boasted of killing in Massachusetts.
>
> Last year, Perry said he had no interest in passing a tough Arizona-style immigration law for his border state. He also has questioned the effectiveness of building a massive border fence, something Romney said . . . should be a priority.

Illegal immigration remains a hot-button issue among Republican activists, but leaders in Texas—where 38 percent of the population is Hispanic—have tended to take a more moderate approach to the issue.

"As governor of Texas, a state that has more than 1,200 miles of border with Mexico, Gov. Perry understands first hand the need to secure our border, something the federal government has failed at," said Perry campaign spokesman Mark Miner. "Because of the federal government's inaction, Texas has spent more than $400 million on border security since 2005. Before you discuss comprehensive immigration reform the border has to be secured."[21]

Perry actually has a politically moderate history with immigration, which many pundits believed could cost any Republican frontrunner the party's nomination. Indeed, few other candidates or persons currently holding political office and addressing undocumented immigration take reasonable stances.

Mitt Romney, the Republican nominee, proposed "self-deportation" as the way to address the immigration issue. In a presidential primary debate, Romney stated that under his plan, life in the United States would become so challenging for undocumented immigrants that they would eventually decide to deport themselves. According to a *Washington Post* editorial,

By declaring that "self-deportation" is the solution to illegal immigration, Mitt Romney gave voice to an idea in wide currency among Republicans that America's 11 million undocumented immigrants would simply go home if government made their lives miserable enough. But even by the debased standards of primary-season rhetoric, the idea is as simpleminded and absurd as it is popular.[22]

Sadly, even the political leaders seeking to challenge the xenophobic tenor of the debate have largely accepted the assertions of the nativists.[23] Consider the comments of Ken Salazar, currently secretary of the interior and a former U.S. senator from Colorado, who disagrees with the tone of the current debate but nevertheless accepts the assertion that America's population is changing in significant ways: "I have no doubt," he said in 2006, "that some of those involved in the debate have their position based on fear and perhaps racism because of what's happening demographically in the country."[24] Like so many others, Salazar accepted without question the assertion that the country is undergoing a major demographic shift caused by undocumented immigrants. At least one Democratic aide more accurately captured the tenor of the attacks: "A lot of the anti-immigration movement is jingoistic at best and racist at worst. There is a fear of white people being overrun by darker-skinned people."[25]

Despite these fairly rare courageous comments, even former Democratic presidential hopefuls have recently shown little sympathy for immigrants. Consider the 2008 attacks on Hillary Clinton, while she was a presidential candidate, after Clinton stated that she understood why a state may want to issue licenses to undocumented immigrants as a tool of identification. Senator Chris Dodd found Clinton's position "troublesome" and doubted that extending the privilege of a driver's license would help with immigration policy.[26]

Many conservative and independent voters in 2008 felt considerable frustration with the government's failure to solve the perceived immigration crisis.[27] According to one report, "illegal immigration ranks as a top concern for many in an electorate increasingly pessimistic about the future."[28] *CBS Evening News* reported that Iowa Republicans felt immigration was the most important issue.[29] *NBC Nightly News* reported that "the immigration debate . . . [was] the core of the [2008] fight for the GOP nomination."[30] The Republican contenders responded accordingly. For instance, in the coverage surrounding a 2008 debate, the former presidential candidates Rudy Giuliani and Mitt Romney attempted to prove how tough they were on immigration. Instead of addressing the issue in an intelligent manner, they exchanged barbs.[31] Romney accused Giuliani of creating a "sanctuary city" out of New York City, and Giuliani attacked Romney for allegedly hiring illegal gardeners.[32]

During the 2008 New Hampshire primary buildup, Romney ran a fifteen-second television ad that twice pointed out Senator John McCain's support of amnesty for undocumented immigrants.[33] The candidate Mike Huckabee similarly took a get-tough stance, "promis[ing] to send undocumented immigrants home."[34] Huckabee remarked, "If illegals cannot find work, they will go back where they belong. . . . I will do everything I can to hasten their trip home by denying them employment."[35] Romney also declared, "The current system puts up a concrete wall to the best and brightest, yet those without skill or education are able to walk across the border."[36]

Other anti-immigrant candidates took the rhetoric a step further. The anti-immigrant group's drum leader warned of the "changing face of America" and how immigrants allegedly posed "a terrorist threat to America." The Republican presidential candidate Tom Tancredo, head of the Immigration Reform Caucus, often invoked the threat of "radical multiculturalism."[37] A 2003 speech before the House of Representatives provides an example of Tancredo's heated rhetoric:

> If we were to actually do what is necessary to prevent people from coming into this country to create havoc and to commit acts of terrorism, we would essentially end illegal immigration. . . . I do not understand how any American, any American regardless of the hyphen, what word we put before the hyphen, I do not understand how any American could say please do not defend our borders because if you do, fewer of my countrymen would be able to come in. Because if you feel that way, then that is your countrymen that we are keeping out, then you are not an American, of course. . . . Then, of course, there are the even more dangerous aspects of this, because the people coming across the border, many of them are carrying drugs, illegal narcotics into the United States. They come with backpacks, 60 to 80 pounds on their back. Sometimes they come guarded by people carrying M-16s or various other automatic weapons. They come across the land in, again, droves, thousands. We have pictures of them.[38]

Tancredo is nothing if not consistent in his high-octane anti-immigrant rhetoric. "They need to be found before it is too late," he said of undocumented immigrants in 2005. "They're coming here to kill you, and you, and me, and my grandchildren."[39] In 2007 Tancredo took hatemongering to new lows in a television ad that equated undocumented immigrants with terrorists.[40]

In what appears to be a competition to see who was toughest on immigration, candidates bantered about sending undocumented immigrants back home, without apparent regard to the devastating impacts such a policy would have on our domestic economy. Perhaps these candidates were really saying, "Damn those immigrants, even if it destroys us!"

Anti-Immigrant Rhetoric by Entertainers

The attacks against the undocumented immigrant community, especially those of Hispanic descent, are not limited to politicians; comedians have adopted similar stances. If these attacks were levied against virtually any other group in this country, a swift and definitive response would surely result, leaving the speaker regretting ever having said the hateful words. However, undocumented immigrants are fair game and can apparently be attacked with little consequence. Consider the tirade launched by the comedian Katt Williams against an audience member who was apparently offended by some of the comedian's comments. Instead of providing a quick response, with some humor, or better yet, an apology, Williams engaged in a hate-infested diatribe. Williams's rant suggests not only some deep-seated venom but also a certain power and privilege to make such racist public comments:

> If y'all had California and you loved it, then you shouldn't have given that mothaf——cka up. You should have fought for California, goddamnit, since you love it. . . .

Are you Mexican? Do you know where Mexico is? No this ain't Mexico, it used to be Mexico, motherf——cker, and now it's Phoenix, goddammit. USA! USA!

F——ck you back, n——gga. I bet you don't even go to Mexico, motha f——cka . . . no n——gga, do you know where you at? USA! USA! I don't give a f——ck. No n——gga, this is my hood. . . . [security comes] F——ck him! Mothaf——ckas think they can live in this country and pledge allegiance to another country . . . do you remember when white people used to say go back to Africa? And we'd have to tell them we don't want to? So if you love Mexico, bitch, get the f——ck over there! [breaks into the National Anthem]. . . . We were slaves bitch, you just all work like that at the landscapers. . . . It's not even racial—you're a bitch! I don't give a f——ck what race that is, that's a p——ssy.[41]

Despite some media coverage and the utter inappropriateness of the comments, Williams did not feel the need to retract them or sincerely apologize. A few days after the incident, Williams told a CNN announcer, "I meant what I said and I said what I meant. . . . I don't think I need to apologize for being pro-American."[42]

Sadly, Williams equates being pro-American with being racist, and to prove his profound ignorance, he uses attacks against African Americans to justify his bigotry. You would think that as an African American he would understand the stupidity of his tirade. He apparently felt no compulsion to retract his statements, even if only for his own financial self-interest. The Williams case demonstrates an utter lack of fear of any consequences to his actions—no fear that his shows or performances would be boycotted, no fear of an outcry. What is even more insulting, instead of public condemnation of his hateful rant, Williams apparently has since been rewarded after his public display of intolerance with a cable television featured special, entitled *Kattpacalypse*, on the Showtime cable network.

Contrast the Williams case with the response to Don Imus for his equally racist description of the Rutgers University women's basketball team as "nappy-headed h——."[43] In announcing his firing, the CBS president, Leslie Moonves, stated,

Those who have spoken with us the last few days represent people of goodwill from all segments of our society—all races, economic groups, men and women alike. In our meetings with concerned groups, there has been much discussion of the effect language like this has on our young people, particularly young women of color trying to make their way in this society. That consideration has weighed most heavily on our minds as we made our decision, as have the many emails, phone calls and personal discussions we have had with our colleagues across the CBS Corporation and our many other constituencies.[44]

While this project does not intend to pit people of color against each other, it uses these events to demonstrate the ease with which some people in this country can attack undocumented immigrants. In particular, Latinos and Latinas are attacked without fear of consequences. Indeed, public outcry, to some extent, is a reflection of social consciousness.

In a situation almost identical to Williams's, the once popular comedian Michael Richards used the hateful "N-word" several times in a bigoted rant in response to a heckler. The reaction to Richards's display of bigotry was swift. Even though Richards apologized, it largely went unaccepted. And as one report recently observed, "Nearly four years later, Richards has failed to regain the public's favor. His career may never rebound."[45]

In another fairly well known incident, the comedian Gilbert Gottfried posted offensive jokes on Twitter concerning the earthquake in Japan, for example, "Japan called me. They said 'maybe those jokes are a hit in the U.S., but over here, they're all sinking'"; and "I was talking to my Japanese real estate agent. I said 'is there a school in this area.' She said 'not now, but just wait.'"[46] Though Gottfried immediately apologized, he was fired from his position as the voice of the Aflac duck, and the company hastened to distance itself from him: "Gilbert's recent comments about the crisis in Japan were lacking in humor and certainly do not represent the thoughts and feelings of anyone at Aflac. . . . There is no place for anything but compassion and concern during these difficult times."[47]

The Media's Hatemongers

The attacks on Latina and Latino immigrants are not only waged by politicians and comedians, but are pervasive in virtually all popular forms of domestic media. Anti-immigrant rhetoric by mainstream media figures has been extensively documented in reports by major advocacy groups and research organizations like the National Hispanic Media Coalition, the National Council of La Raza, the Southern Poverty Law Center, the Leadership Conference, and the Anti-Defamation League (ADL). These supporters of civil rights and immigration reform have also scrutinized the media's role in shaping public opinion and have raised important questions about cable news conglomerates and why they select, advertise, and actively market spokespersons who openly advocate racially insensitive positions.[48] Moreover, the National Hispanic Media Coalition (NHMC) "has undertaken a study to quantify the hate speech in commercial radio, petitioned the Federal Communications Commission (FCC) to open an inquiry into hate speech on the nation's airwaves, and requested that the National Telecommunications and Information Administration (NTIA) update its 1993 report, The Role of Telecommunications in Hate Crime."[49]

Alarmingly, hateful anti-immigrant rhetoric is spewed by media personalities with mainstream national exposure, such as John Gibson, Neal Boortz, Michael Savage, Bill O'Reilly, Pat Buchanan, and, perhaps most notoriously, Lou Dobbs.

In 2006 John Gibson implored his Fox News viewers to "do your duty. Make more babies . . . half of the kids in this country under five years old are minorities. By far the greatest numbers are Hispanic. You know what that means? Twenty-five years and the majority of the population is Hispanic."[50] Comments like these are damaging not only because they are inaccurate, but because, like prejudicial evidence in a courtroom, once the damning statement's impact is felt, its accuracy becomes largely irrelevant. Those who heard Gibson's claim that half of America will soon be Hispanic had most likely not seen the census data that would have refuted him; otherwise they would know that by 2030, the Hispanic population in the United States will be approximately 20 percent of the overall population—a far cry from the majority takeover Gibson alleges. In fact, forty years from now the majority of Americans will still be white, and the Hispanic population will only be approaching 24 percent.[51]

Media figures such as the Fox News talk show host Bill O'Reilly have proclaimed that the supporters of immigration reform "hate America" and "want to flood the country with foreign nationals . . . to change the complexion . . . of America."[52] The radio talk show host Neal Boortz declared that "what the American people want [is] . . . to build a double fence along the Mexican border, and stop the damn invasion. I don't care if Mexicans pile up against that fence like tumbleweeds. . . . Let 'em. . . . then just run a couple of taco trucks up and down the line, and somebody's gonna be a millionaire out of that."[53] Yet another nativist radio host, Michael Savage, has alleged that the civil rights organization La Raza is "the Ku Klux Klan of the Hispanic People."[54] Interestingly, according to reports, Savage has been barred since 2009 from entering the United Kingdom for allegedly "seeking to provoke others to serious criminal acts and fostering hatred."[55]

A comment by Savage in 2007 provides a good example of another tactic used by anti-immigrant media figures: depicting undocumented immigrants as criminals.

> Then there's the story of college students who are fasting out here in the Bay Area. They're illegal aliens and they want green cards simply because they're students. . . . I would say, let them fast until they starve to death, then that solves the problem. Because then we won't have a problem about giving them green cards because they're illegal aliens; they don't belong here to begin with. They broke into the country; they're criminals.[56]

The truth is that crossing the border without appropriate documentation is a misdemeanor under U.S. federal law; consequently, undocumented immigrants are not anywhere near criminals as the hatemongers suggest.

In a report by the Anti-Defamation League, the views of the former presidential candidate and paleoconservative political commentator Pat Buchanan were compared to that of white supremacists. According to the ADL report, Buchanan "derides what he alleges are . . . [the] differences between non-white immigrants and white Americans, which he believes threaten to alter the 'character' of the United States. . . . One of Buchanan's most widely-employed arguments is that undocumented immigrants, specifically those from Mexico are secretly plotting 'La Reconquista,' a conspiracy to 'invade' the United States and conquer its Southwestern territory, also referred to as 'Aztlan.'" Buchanan describes the "Aztlan Strategy" as

> endless migration from Mexico north, the Hispanicization of the American Southwest, and dual citizenship for all Mexican-Americans. The goals: Erase the border. Grow the influence, through Mexican-Americans, over how America disposes of her wealth and power. Gradually circumscribe the sovereignty of the United States. Lastly, economic and political merger of the nations in a bi-national union. And in the nuptial agreement, a commitment to share the wealth and power. Stated bluntly, the Aztlan Strategy entails the end of a sovereign, self-sufficient, independent republic, the passing away of the American nation. They are coming to conquer us.[57]

Perhaps the most notorious anti-immigrant media figure is Lou Dobbs, a longtime CNN anchor who is now with the Fox Business Network. Dobbs has repeatedly warned against an "illegal alien invasion"[58] and has stated unequivocally, "illegal aliens are criminals."[59] A report from the Southern Poverty Law Center, "Getting Immigration Facts Straight," cites a claim made on Dobbs's show as an example of anti-immigrant rhetoric that is blindly accepted as fact:

> A case in point is the 2005 claim made by CNN's "Lou Dobbs Tonight" show that 7,000 cases of leprosy had been reported in the United States

in a recent three-year period—one of the "deadly imports," in Dobbs' words, that immigration brings. . . . These kinds of facts generally originate with modern nativist groups and ideologues . . . or even unabashedly race-based hate groups, but that has not stopped them from making their way, often by force of sheer repetition, into mainstream venues like "Lou Dobbs Tonight."[60]

The National Council of La Raza has documented many examples of Dobbs's anti-immigrant hostility:

- Dobbs has used the term "anchor babies" to refer to the U.S.-born children of undocumented immigrants, suggesting inaccurately that having a U.S. citizen child is a means of acquiring legal immigration status or being protected from deportation. (*Lou Dobbs Tonight* transcript, 3/31/05).
- Dobbs refers frequently to illegal aliens from Mexico into the United States as the "invasion" and as an "army of invaders" (*Lou Dobbs Tonight* transcript, 3/31/06). One of his reporters referred to a visit from Mexico's then-President Vicente Fox as a "Mexican military incursion."
- Dobbs linked illegal aliens to a host of diseases including tuberculosis, malaria, and leprosy. In 2005, a reporter on the show claimed that there had been 7,000 new cases of leprosy in the previous three years (*Lou Dobbs Tonight* transcript, 4/14/05). This claim has been disputed by the Centers for Disease Control and Prevention. To date, and despite protests to the contrary, Dobbs has never acknowledged the error on his show.
- Dobbs has featured several stories on Lou Dobbs Tonight concerning the "reconquest" of the American Southwest. In one 2005 segment, a map purportedly showing "Aztlan" was provided to the show by the Council of Conservative Citizens, a prominent White supremacist organization (*Lou Dobbs Tonight* transcript, 5/23/06).
- Dobbs has also been a cheerleader for the Minuteman Project. He devoted extensive coverage to the Minuteman's first action in 2005, calling the group a "remarkable success." Minuteman leaders were frequent guests on *Lou Dobbs Tonight*, and on one occasion Dobbs wished one "all the success in the world."

- Dobbs featured on *Lou Dobbs Tonight* the late Madeline Cosman as a "medical expert" in a discussion of the diseases that illegal aliens are bringing into the country. Ms. Cosman was not a medical doctor, but a prominent anti-immigrant activist who stated that Mexican immigrants were prone to molesting children (*Lou Dobbs Tonight* transcript, 6/8/05).
- As noted above, the Council of Conservative Citizens, one of the most well-known White supremacist groups in the country, was featured as a "source" in a 2006 segment on the show.[61]

Despite their obvious and simplistic demagoguery, leaders of the anti-immigration agenda have had their impact on the national stage. For instance, the failure of comprehensive immigration reform before Congress in 2006 has been largely attributed to the effect of conservative talk show hosts' calls for massive telephone campaigns directed at congressional leaders in order to kill immigration reform.[62] According to Nancy Pelosi, then Speaker of the House of Representatives, "talk radio, or in some cases hate radio . . . just go on and on in a xenophobic, anti-immigrant manner."[63] Senator John McCain, one of the sponsors of a moderate comprehensive reform bill, initially supported reform that would include a guest worker program and a path for undocumented workers to achieve citizenship.[64] However, succumbing to the outcry against such reform, McCain changed his position on the matter, and shortly after becoming the Republican presidential nominee in 2008, advocated for an "enforcement first" approach to immigration.[65]

In addition, the media's fearmongering about the "browning" of America clearly has found an audience among some sectors of the American people. The *Washington Post* recently profiled the views of the so-called average American. One interviewee stated that she stopped shopping at Wal-Mart because she "noticed she was the only non-Latino customer" in the store: "I'm in the minority, and if we don't get control over this, pretty soon all of America will be outnumbered." Another interviewee reportedly complained that Latinos had turned his neighborhood into "a slum."[66]

The New Nativists

Perhaps it is no surprise that anti-immigrant hate speech is generated by extremist vigilante organizations, many of which have been publicly denounced by the mainstream political parties.[67] For instance, according to the Southern Poverty Law Center, Glenn Spencer, leader of the anti-immigration group American Patrol, operates a website filled with anti-Mexican rhetoric and accuses the Mexican government of secretly plotting to take back the southwest United States.[68] Another vocal advocate warning of the "immigration invasion" is Joe McCutchen, leader of Project Arkansas Now and author of numerous anti-Semitic letters to the editors of local newspapers, whose extremism was denounced by the Republican governor of his state.[69] Yet another vocal anti-immigrant organizer is Jim Gilchrist, founder of the Minuteman Project, an armed militia that purportedly attempts to engage in Border Patrol–like policing. According to the Campaign for a United America, Gilchrist's statements and tactics "have drawn denunciations from faith leaders, human rights activists and even President Bush[,] who called Gilchrist and his shotgun-toting posse vigilantes. . . . Gilchrist allowed members of the National Alliance, one of the United States' largest neo-Nazi organizations, to help with his 2005 campaign for the U.S. House of Representatives."[70]

Such groups operate on the fringes, and always have. But in an alarming development in recent years, some extremist anti-immigrant groups are presenting themselves as mainstream, and are given widespread media coverage. In its 2009 report "The Nativist Lobby: Three Faces of Intolerance," the Southern Poverty Law Center analyzed three organizations that it describes as "the nexus of the American nativist movement": the Federation for American Immigration Reform (FAIR), the Center for Immigration Studies (CIS), and NumbersUSA, "part of a network of restrictionist organizations conceived and created by John Tanton, the 'puppeteer' of the nativist movement and a man with deep racist roots."[71] The report documents the intricate connections between these supposedly unrelated groups, and also details Tanton's racist history, his support for eugenics, and his conspiracy theories about a Latino take-over of the United States. What is most remarkable and disturbing is the amount of mainstream acceptance these organizations, especially FAIR, have achieved:

> None of [the evidence for] the bigotry and racism that courses through the group seems to have affected FAIR's media standing. In 2008, the group was quoted in mainstream media outlets nearly 500 times. FAIR staff has been featured several times on CNN's "Lou Dobbs Tonight," along with countless appearances on other television news shows. Dobbs even ran his radio program from a FAIR event in Washington, D.C. this past September [2008]. And, perhaps most remarkably of all, FAIR has been taken seriously by Congress, claiming on its home page that it has been asked to testify on immigration bills "more than any other organization in America."[72]

According to the 2008 Anti-Defamation League report "Immigrants Targeted: Extremist Rhetoric Moves into the Mainstream," extremist anti-immigrant organizations "are frequently quoted in the media, have been called to testify before Congress, and often hold meetings with lawmakers and other public figures. However, under the guise of warning people about the impact of illegal immigration, anti-immigrant advocates often invoke the same dehumanizing, racist stereotypes as hate groups. And increasingly, they do not make a distinction between illegal and legal immigrants."[73] Of particular interest, yet virtually unnoticed in mainstream media, the ADL report drew conclusions similar to those that will be explored in detail in this book:

> A closer look at the public record reveals that some . . . supposedly mainstream organizations have disturbing links to, or relationships with, extremists in the anti-immigration movement. Often identified in the media or their mission statements as "anti–illegal immigration advocacy groups," they attempt to distort the debate over immigration by fomenting fear and spreading unfounded propaganda through the use of several key tactics:

- Describing immigrants as "third world invaders," who come to America to destroy our heritage, "colonize" the country and attack our "way of life."
- Using terminology that describes immigrants as part of "hordes" that "swarm" over the border.
- Portraying immigrants as carriers of diseases like leprosy, tuberculosis, Chagas disease, dengue fever, polio, and malaria.
- Depicting immigrants as criminals, murderers, rapists, terrorists, and a danger to children and families.
- Propagating conspiracy theories about an alleged secret "Reconquista" plot by Mexican immigrants to create a "greater Mexico" by seizing seven states in the American Southwest that once belonged to Mexico.
- Blaming immigrants for eroding American Culture, institutions and quality of life and impacting our environment and natural resources.[74]

The Resulting Violence

Regrettably, too many individuals in our society fail to recognize that hateful, irresponsible anti-immigrant rhetoric has consequences. As the Leadership Conference notes, "There is a direct connection between the tenor of this rhetoric and the daily lives of immigrants, and many fear that the unintended consequence of media celebrities vilifying immigrants will be an atmosphere in which some people will act on these demonizing screeds, violently targeting immigrants and those perceived to be immigrants."[75] There are, unfortunately, many examples of violence against immigrants. I will mention here only a handful.

For instance, during the summer of 2011, a Molotov cocktail was thrown at an immigrant rights advocate's home in Racine, Wisconsin. The attack was believed to be in retaliation after the woman, Maria Morales, and her advocacy group, Voces de la Frontera, objected to a local gas station's sale of bumper stickers depicting an "illegal immigrant hunting permit." The group asked the gas station owner to stop selling the bumper stickers. Shortly thereafter, the attack occurred. Fortunately there were no injuries.[76]

According to a federal report released in 2010, an inquiry from the Transportation Security Administration found that TSA workers at Newark Liberty International Airport used racial profiling to pull aside travelers. Despite regulations requiring detection of suspicious behavior, these security officers regularly singled out Mexican or Dominican passengers and sent them to immigration officials based on made-up behavioral irregularities. The practice became a running joke at the airport and managers even condoned the behavior, calling the workers "the great Mexican hunters."[77]

The vitriolic rhetoric has led to repeated attacks against individuals, who because they appear to be Latino or Latina, are automatically deemed to be undocumented immigrants. For example, in New York, an Ecuadorian immigrant named Marcelo Lucero was fatally stabbed in November 2008 by Jeffrey Conroy. Lucero's attackers testified that "targeting Hispanics was something they did 'for kicks' [because they were] confident their victims would not call police" due to their fear of "questions about their immigration status."[78] Since the stabbing, community leaders such as Gilda Ramos have been campaigning for local law enforcement to increase their vigilance when it comes to hate crimes against immigrants. Ramos said that attackers view immigrants as "walking ATM's" because the victims are often "robbed on Friday or Saturday night after getting paid from jobs such as dishwashing, construction or landscaping." Community leaders agree that in order to reduce the number of hate crimes in the community, local officials must make it easier for immigrants to report attacks.[79] Ultimately, Conroy was convicted of manslaughter, and the incident was designated a hate crime. Six other teenagers were also implicated.[80]

In 2010, also in New York, police investigated a string of at least ten alleged hate crimes in Staten Island's Port Richmond neighborhood, all of which were violent assaults perpetrated against Mexicans, during which the attackers yelled anti-Mexican slurs. Residents say that previous attacks date back to 2003, and police believe that many go unreported every year.[81]

Hate crime charges were also brought in a 2010 case in San Francisco, when, according to CBS News, "five men yelled 'white power' and made racist comments while attacking two Hispanic men near a Tenderloin bar. . . . The group assaulted one victim from behind, knocking him to the ground and punching and kicking him in the face until he blacked out. . . . The second victim tried to intervene and was also attacked. Both men survived, but one was hospitalized."[82] San Francisco's district attorney saw the attack as part of a larger pattern of an increase in hate crimes in the city.[83]

Anti-immigrant vigilantes were convicted of the murder of a nine-year-old girl and her father in Arizona in 2009. Shawna Forde and two accomplices raided the home of Raul Flores; they had "posed as immigration agents and pushed their way through the door. She and her accomplices . . . allegedly shot Raul Flores before turning their guns on Brisenia [his daughter], who begged not to be shot."[84] Forde's background as an anti-immigrant zealot is of particular interest. As reported in the *Huffington Post*, Forde

> once maintained a Tea Party blog, was a member of Minuteman Civil Defense Corps and has presented herself as a representative of Federation for American Immigration Reform. (All three have since distanced themselves from her.) After being cast out from the Minuteman group due to erratic behavior, she formed her own vigilante group, called Minutemen American Defense, which also patrolled the United States–Mexico border trying to detect illegal immigration.[85]

An atmosphere of anti-immigrant hostility was an important factor in the brutal beating death of Luis Eduardo Ramirez Zavala, a Mexican immigrant in Shenandoah, Pennsylvania, in 2008. As detailed in the Leadership Conference's report "Confronting the New Faces of Hate,"

> Ramirez, a 25 year-old Mexican and father of two, was murdered because of his ethnicity in a brutal beating allegedly by four current and former high school football players. The teenagers reportedly yelled, "This is Shenandoah, this is America, go back to Mexico," as well as ethnic slurs. They then repeatedly punched Ramirez, knocking him to the ground, and

then kicked him multiple times in the head. As Ramirez lay unconscious, convulsing and foaming at the mouth, one of the assailants reportedly yelled "Tell your fucking Mexican friends to get the fuck out of Shenandoah or you'll be fucking laying next to them."[86]

Local officials, including several police officers from the area, were also indicted for obstruction of justice: it is alleged that some of the officers helped the men "concoct a story and cover up what really happened."[87] Tensions in the town were believed to be the build-up to the attack. Supposedly, parents were not happy with having to send their kids to school with immigrants, and their children picked up on the sentiment.[88]

This brutal murder occurred the year after nearby Hazleton, Pennsylvania, passed an "Illegal Immigrant Relief Act," which "sought to suspend the permits of local businesses and others for employing 'unlawful workers' and landlords for renting to 'illegal aliens.'"[89] Lou Dobbs praised Hazleton for the ordinance and in fact solicited donations on his website for Hazleton's legal defense after the ordinance was challenged in court by MALDEF and the ACLU.[90] According to the report by the Leadership Conference,

> the Hazelton ordinance caused considerable tension between [Shenandoah's] Hispanic and white communities, which had formerly enjoyed peaceful relations. . . . As *The New York Times* reported, "Many people believe the debate fueled by Hazleton's actions helped create the environment that led to Mr. Ramirez's death." "Clearly there were a lot of factors here," said Gladys Limón, a lawyer for MALDEF. "But I do believe that the inflammatory rhetoric in the immigration debate does have a correlation with increased violence against Latinos."[91]

Unfortunately, violent attacks against those perceived as immigrants are not rare, and in fact are increasing. *Trans-Border News*, for example, reports that

> since 2010, at least 10 Mexicans have been killed or seriously injured as a result of a hate crime, according to Daniel Hernandez Joseph of [Mexico's]

State Department office for the Protection of Mexicans Abroad. . . . The number of hate crimes against Mexicans has been increasing in the past 8 years, with 19 of the 24 cases occurring after 2008. . . . Hernandez believed that number to be in fact higher, but officially in the American courts, "It is very hard to obtain the hate crime classification." . . .

Hernandez went on to opine that the spike in hate crimes against Hispanics, whether citizens or immigrants, is a result of increased debate and stricter legislation regarding immigration in the United States, with 600 new initiatives in January 2011. Anti-immigration laws treat the undocumented immigrant as a criminal, said Hernandez, which allows for society's abuse.[92]

Similarly, the Leadership Conference's "Confronting the New Faces of Hate" report cited FBI statistics (see figure 2.1) to conclude that

the increase in hate crimes directed against Hispanics for the fourth consecutive year is particularly noteworthy and worrisome because the number of hate crimes committed against other racial, ethnic, and religious groups has over the same period shown either no increase or a decrease.

The increase in violence against Hispanics correlates closely with the increasingly heated debate over Comprehensive Immigration Reform and an escalation in the level of anti-immigrant vitriol on radio, television, and the Internet.[93]

The report also quoted an "assessment from the Office of Intelligence and Analysis at the U.S. Department of Homeland Security (DHS)[:] 'in some cases, anti-Immigration or strident pro-enforcement fervor has been directed against specific groups and has the potential to turn violent.'"[94] This potential, as we have seen, is already being realized.

Some Provocative Questions

A terribly troubling aspect of the current anti-immigrant attacks is that the assertions of the nativists are not only misguided, but false.[95] Given

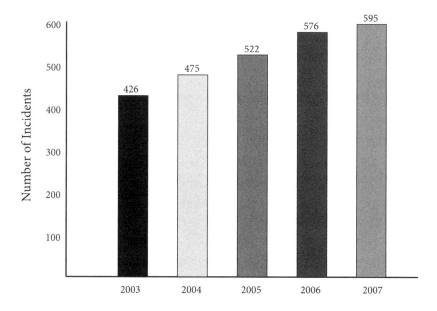

Figure 2.1. Anti-hispanic hate crime incidents. Source: FBI data.

the frequency of these errors, one must question whether they are made with knowledge of their inaccuracy.[96] Another question that needs to be asked is why the anti-immigrant claims go largely unchallenged in the national media. This book therefore will attempt to engage in what the public discourse has thus far largely failed to do—challenge the three basic premises associated with the so-called illegal immigration invasion. Despite the hateful rhetoric used by so many, an examination of the leading empirical studies demonstrates that the demagogues are wrong with respect to all three of their basic premises: (1) that there is an "invasion" of illegal immigrants; (2) that the invasion will lead to devastating economic harm to the country; and (3) that unprecedented crime will accompany this illegal invasion.

Perhaps the most amazing aspect of what appear to be widespread attacks against undocumented immigrants levied by politicians, performers, and media leaders is that the anti-immigrant movement's irresponsible and outlandish attacks have thus far not provoked mass outrage and scorn. Are Latinos and Latinas less deserving of respect and dignity? If racist statements were made against Asian Americans, African Americans, or other racial or ethnic minorities, would the comments become acceptable if the focus of the particular attacks was on noncitizens? As one national columnist observed, "While the 44 million Hispanics are the biggest minority in America, you don't see the kind of nationwide protests, legal actions or calls for boycotts on a scale you would probably see if these statements were directed against African Americans or Jewish Americans."[97] Is it not time for this land's Latino people, other people of color, and like-minded whites to call for an end to the intolerably racist and largely inaccurate attacks?[98] Perhaps more importantly, the tenor of the current debate confuses the masses, distracts them from legitimate concerns over the impact of immigration on local and state economies, and unfairly polarizes both sides of the immigration debate. The goal of this project and related ones is to deflate the force of bias as part of a goal to open the door to legitimate dialogue and analysis.

Instead of honest, fact-based undertakings and forceful but responsible reactions, at best what tends to occur are ever-so-cautious suggestions that some of the current anti-Latino attacks are insensitive or touch upon race. Frustrations stemming from such cautious critiques raise inevitable questions: Is it so difficult to call a bigot a bigot when the attacks are aimed at Spanish-speaking people? Why do so many fail to challenge attacks filled with baseless stereotypes and false assertions? Are all accusations and insults acceptable merely because they occur in the name of protecting America's borders or Anglo-American culture?[99] For instance, a *Time* magazine article on increased interest in immigration ever-so-gently noted that race may play a part in the current debate: "The Democratic allegations of racism may sound like just another political ploy, but there certainly is a case to be made that racial fears are informing some of the debate on immigration policy."[100] The article nevertheless raised a far more telling irony, namely, that while national security is typically the basis for proposing closing our southern border, "why . . . is no one proposing sending additional National Guard Troops to secure the U.S.-Canada border?"[101] The question is not unreasonable, particularly because while Ahmed Ressam, also known as the "Millennium Bomber," was caught at the Canadian border, none of the nineteen September 11th terrorists entered at the Mexican border.[102]

The following chapter examines the leading studies on the effects of recent immigration, which discredit the xenophobes. In chapter 4 the objections to immigration often made at the state or local level will be examined. This is followed by chapter 5, which provides an overview of this country's long history of anti-immigrant efforts. Subsequently, chapter 6 engages in a sociological and psychological examination of the anti-immigrant efforts, and discusses how such views continue to lead to perceptions as well as policy decisions that negatively affect both immigrant communities and the country as a whole. The book ends by providing sound policy reasons for engaging in honest, fact-based debates and decision making concerning immigration. It also hopefully provides reasons for following the proposed solutions herein. And finally, it provides a pragmatic political reason for why the tenor of the debate will inevitably change.

3

Empirical Data on Immigration

America's immigration system is outdated, unsuited to the
needs of our economy and to the values of our country. We
should not be content with laws that punish hard-working
people and deny businesses willing workers and invite chaos
at our border.
—President George W. Bush, February 2, 2005

[I] believe our immigration policy should be driven by our
best judgment of what is in the economic interest of the
United States and what is in the best interest of the American
worker. . . . [I, as president of the United States,] recognize
that an orderly controlled border and an immigration system
designed to meet our economic needs are important pillars
of a healthy and robust economy.
—President Barack Obama, January 10, 2010

Perhaps no issue related to the immigration debate is touted more as
fact than the so-called economic consequences of undocumented immigration. Time and time again politicians, news pundits, and the occa-
sional academic advance arguments concerning the negative impact
of undocumented immigrants on our economy. With often little more
than conjecture or individualized anecdotes to support their sweeping
conclusions, commentators weigh in on the presumed consequences

of "illegal" immigration, including a supposed population explosion, a purported increase in crime, and—perhaps most damning—the supposed drain on our economy.

I am not contending that all arguments to limit immigration are solely or in any major way motivated by racial hostility toward minorities in general and ethnic immigrants in particular. For instance, opposition to driver's licenses for undocumented workers may come across as racially motivated, but could also easily be motivated by a legitimate concern for the rule of law.[1]

In terms of the economic consequences of immigration, the typical arguments include accusations that undocumented immigrants (1) take jobs away from domestic workers; (2) drive down wages for domestic workers; and (3) constitute a drain on the national economy—creating massive costs domestically in terms of healthcare, education, and additional expenditures associated with crime prevention and incarceration. While data on these topics are often quite fluid, this chapter attempts to compile the leading works on these subjects. In such a contestatory and ever-changing setting, an attempt to rise above the cacophony of views is difficult, if not impossible; nonetheless, this chapter attempts to engage in an honest and in-depth analysis of the issues that are at the heart of a political stalemate in this country.

The Alleged Invasion

In his book *The Latino Threat*, the noted immigration scholar Leo Chavez observes that while the stereotype of the Mexican criminal was widely disseminated throughout the last century, since the 1970s "a new trope was added: Mexican immigration as an invasion of the United States."[2] Assertions of an overthrow inundate the airwaves with little or no evidence to support them. Among the examples cited by the Southern Poverty Law Center is the "Heritage Foundation senior fellow Robert Rector, [who] . . . said [in 2006] that the proposed Kennedy-McCain immigration reform bill would likely result in 103 million legal immigrants in the next 20 years. He added that the maximum number in that period could reach 200 million people."[3]

Claims like these are not only unsupported by the facts, but also contrary to logic. For one, the entire population of Mexico is about 115 million.[4] In order for 200 million people to immigrate to the United States, the entire population of Mexico and Central America would have to relocate.[5] In fact, Rector's estimates were criticized by prominent demographers as well as by the Congressional Budget Office, which "estimated that the [proposed Kennedy-McCain] bill would have resulted in 8 million people entering the country legally over 20 years."[6]

In the 1990s the Cato Institute, a libertarian think tank that has undertaken numerous studies on immigration, reported that immigrant population statistics, in terms of real numbers, were in no way approaching what the alarmists have described as an explosion, as shown in the charts reproduced here in figures 3.1 and 3.2.

According to the Cato report,

The numbers of aliens illegally residing and working in the United States at present (the "stock" of nondocumented persons) as well as the number by which the stock is increased each year (the net "flow" of nondocumented persons) enter importantly into the discussion of immigration. In the past when there was slight knowledge of these subjects, huge numbers were bandied about; for example, the Immigration and Naturalization Service has publicized estimates as high as 12 million residents. By now, however, demographers have a rather solid understanding of how many illegals are in the United States and have now reached reasonable consensus. (Some of the major methods include analyses of death registrations, census data, Mexican census data, and surveys of Mexican villages.) . . .

According to an authoritative recent review, the net flow "is 200,000 to 300,000 a year" (Fix and Passel 1994, 4). This estimate is of the same order (though perhaps a bit lower) than the 305,000 net annual addition that was estimated for 1989 to 1992 by Robert Warren of the INS (another main long-time student of the subject), a number which itself reflects a "modest drop" from the 334,000 estimated for the period 1982–1988

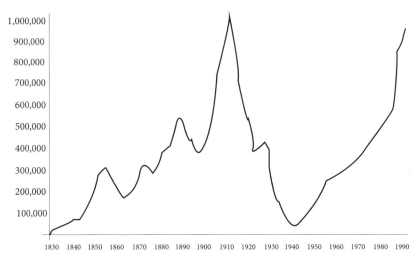

Figure 3.1. Average number of U.S. immigrants from 1830–1993. This graph shows that in absolute numbers, the rate of immigration was roughly the same at the turn of the century as at present, even allowing for the illegal immigrants who were admitted by amnesty at the turn of the recent decade. Source: Julian L. Simon, *Immigration: The Demographic and Economic Facts* (Washington, DC: Cato Institute and National Immigration Forum, 1995). Reprinted by permission.

(correspondence, August 31, 1993). A modest interpretation of these data is not that they show a decline but that they show the absence of an important increase.[7]

The Cato study looked at immigration in terms of overall U.S. population and demonstrated that the rate of undocumented immigration is at one of its lowest levels, as shown in figure 3.3.

In the mid-1990s the National Research Council convened a panel of demographers, economists, and sociologists at the request of Congress's bipartisan Commission on Immigration Reform. In 1997 and 1998 the Panel on the Demographic and Economic Impacts of Immigration published its report in two volumes, *The New Americans* and *The Immigration Debate*, considered the most comprehensive empirical examination of the issue (I will refer to the two volumes collectively as the "NRC report"). Not surprisingly, the NRC report refutes the "alien invasion"

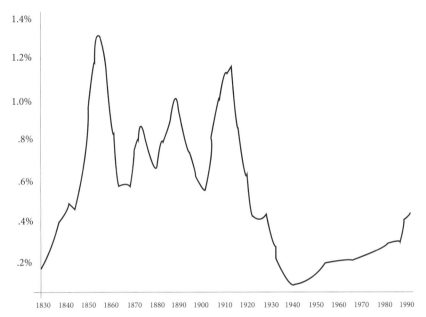

Figure 3.2. Ten-year moving average rate of immigration, 1830–1993. This graph shows the 10-year moving average of the number of new immigrants relative to the size of the population. The rate of immigration in the most recent decade is about one-third the rate at the previous peak at the turn of the century. Source: Julian L. Simon, *Immigration: The Demographic and Economic Facts* (Washington, DC: CATO Institute and National Immigration Forum, 1995). Reprinted by permission.

rhetoric: "Although the absolute number of current immigrants rivals the peak levels at the beginning of the twentieth century, expressed relative to the size of the existing U.S. population, current immigration is far more modest."[8] Another chapter in the NRC report reaches similar conclusions: "Immigrant flows were larger in the past."[9]

> To put the current immigration flows into proper perspective . . . [o]ur calculations reveal that, in proportionate terms, the current inflow of immigrants is rather modest. . . . If we look only at the "regular" immigrants—that is, exclusive of those admitted under the IRCA—then the current inflows approximate those in the very slowest years from the period between 1840 and the onset of World War I. . . . Only the disruptions of

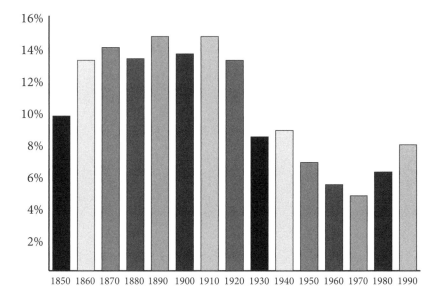

Figure 3.3. Immigrants as a percentage of the population, 1850–1990. This graph shows that the proportion of the U.S. population that was born abroad is lower in the 1990s than in any decade from the middle of the 19th century until the 1950s. Source: Julian L. Simon, *Immigration: The Demographic and Economic Facts* (Washington, DC: CATO Institute and National Immigration Forum, 1995). Reprinted by permission.

World War I pushed the flow of immigrants relative to the native population to levels below the relatively low levels that we experience today.[10]

The authors concluded that the number of the foreign-born living in the United States, as a percentage of the total population, was higher for each year from 1850 to 1930 than it was for 1990.[11]

A more recent study published by the Cato Institute's Center for Trade Policy Studies affirms these conclusions, as shown in figure 3.4.[12]

There are less reputable studies suggesting that immigration is at high levels. In 2007 the *New York Times* reported on a study by the Center for Immigration Studies that found that legal and illegal immigration "over the past seven years was the highest for any seven-year period in American history." The *Times* article, however, quoted many other experts who refuted this finding, including a 2005 report by the Pew Hispanic Center.

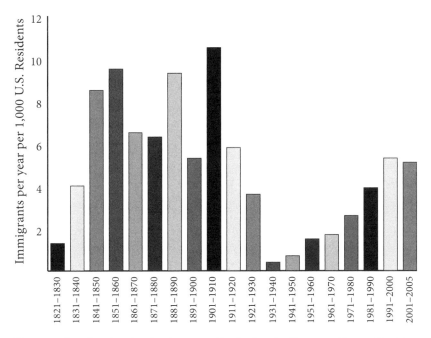

Figure 3.4. American immigration in perspective, by decade, 1820–2005. Source: Daniel Griswold, "Comprehensive Immigration Reform: Finally Getting It Right," Center for Free Trade Policy Studies, May 16, 2007. Data from U.S. Census Bureau; *2005 Yearbook of Immigration Statistics*, U.S. Office of Immigration Statistics; and Pew Hispanic Center. Reprinted by permission.

In addition, Dowell Myers, a demographer at the University of Southern California, called the study a "one-eyed portrait," and Wayne Cornelius, a University of California political science professor, called the study's conclusions "misleading."[13]

A 2010 report for the Pew Hispanic Center similarly looked to the issue of population rates of immigration, and like the other studies cited in this section, found that the claims of a mass invasion or alleged population overthrow are simply not supported by the data and in fact, immigration rates have actually gone down in the last decade (see figure 3.5): "The annual inflow of unauthorized immigrants to the United States was nearly two-thirds smaller in the March 2007 to March 2009 period than it had been from March 2000 to March 2005."[14]

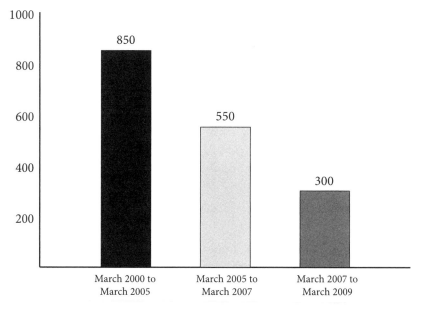

Figure 3.5. Average annual inflow of unauthorized immigrants to the U.S., in thousands, by period, 2000–2009. Source: Jeffrey S. Passel and D'Vera Cohn, "U.S. Unauthorized Immigration Flows Are Down Sharply Since Mid-Decade," Pew Hispanic Center, September 1, 2010. Reprinted by permission.

Recent commentators have also noted that immigration declines during a recession; thus, warnings about an alleged invasion are even less relevant in the current economic climate. Figure 3.6 shows the decrease in Border Patrol apprehensions along the U.S.-Mexico border during times of recession.

There is simply no empirical basis for the hysteria over a "broken" immigration system and a "mass invasion" that will change the face of America. Study after study has demonstrated that despite the widespread alarmist rhetoric, immigration rates are in fact low.

The Alleged Crime Wave

In my discussion of the supposed connection between immigrants and crime, I draw on several well-respected sources: the Migration Policy

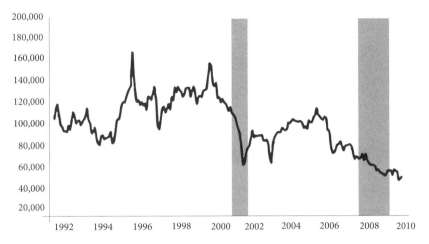

Figure 3.6. Reduced number of migrant apprehensions along U.S.-Mexico border during recessions, seasonally adjusted. Shaded bars indicate U.S. recessions. Source: Mike Nicholson and Pia Orrenius, "Manning the Gates: Migration Policy in the Great Recession," Federal Reserve Bank of Dallas, Economic Letter, vol. 5, no. 5, June 2010. Data from U.S. Border Patrol. Reprinted by permission.

Institute, the Public Policy Institute of California, the Southern Poverty Law Center, and ProCon.org.

In "Getting Immigration Facts Straight," her 2007 report for the Southern Poverty Law Center, Heidi Beirich provides disturbing examples of anti-immigrant activists hurling unsupported allegations of crime waves:

> U.S. Rep. Steve King (R-Iowa), in a May 5, 2006, column on his website, claimed that a day without immigrants would create a far safer America: "The lives of 12 U.S. citizens would be saved who otherwise die a violent death at the hands of murderous illegal aliens each day. Another 13 Americans would survive who are otherwise killed each day by uninsured drunk driving illegals." King's claim has been repeated hundreds of times, sometimes by extremist activists like Clyde Harkins of the American Constitution Party, and frequently by radio hosts like Peter Boyles of Denver's KHOW-AM. Boyles also suggested last year

that illegal immigrants had murdered 45,000 American citizens since Sept. 11, 2001.

King claimed he had "extrapolated" his numbers from a study by the General Accounting Office, Congress' nonpartisan investigative arm, that he said showed 28% of inmates in local jails and state and federal prisons were "criminal aliens." What the GAO study actually showed was that 28% of all federal prisoners (federal prisoners make up 12%-17% of the total incarcerated population in the U.S.) were either legal or illegal immigrants. . . . It also stated that about 50% of those immigrants were only charged with being in the country illegally, a federal misdemeanor. Just 12% of the total in federal custody were there for murder, rape, robbery or other violent crimes. Regarding the claim of 45,000 Americans murdered by illegal immigrants, FBI statistics show some 85,000 murders from 9/11 to the end of 2006. If the claim by Boyles and others were true, that would mean undocumented immigrants, who make up under 4% of the U.S. population, were responsible for 53% of all murders.[15]

In 2008 the nonprofit, nonpartisan organization ProCon.org devoted an article to a roundup of answers to the question, "Does illegal immigration relate to higher crime incidence?" It provides an interesting sampling of rhetoric about the supposed criminality of immigrants, for example, this claim from the Federation for American Immigration Reform (FAIR), a self-proclaimed mainstream immigration organization:

Most Americans equate illegal aliens with a higher incidence of crime. . . . Adult illegal aliens represented 3.1 percent of the total adult population of the country in 2003. By comparison, the illegal alien prison population represented a bit more than 4.54 percent of the overall prison population. Therefore, deportable criminal aliens were more than half again as likely to be incarcerated as their share of the population. . . . Those who sneak into the country undergo no form of screening for criminality or any other grounds for exclusion. . . . illegal aliens . . . end up being co-opted into criminal activity.[16]

Another source of irresponsible hyperbole is Deborah Schurman-Kauflin, founder of the Violent Crimes Institute, who equated illegal immigrants with sexual predators:

> After conducting a 12 month in-depth study of illegal immigrants who committed sex crimes and murders for the time period of January 1999 through April 2006, it is clear that the U.S. public faces a dangerous threat from sex predators who cross the U.S. borders illegally . . . most of the offenders were located in states with the highest numbers of illegal immigrants. . . . There is a clear pattern of criminal escalation. From misdemeanors such as assault or DUI, to drug offenses, illegal immigrants who commit sex crimes break U.S. laws repeatedly. . . . Their attacks are particularly brutal, and they use a hands-on method of controlling and/ or killing their victims.[17]

And consider these charges bandied about by a group called Family Security Matters, in a 2007 article entitled "Illegal Aliens Kill More Americans Than Iraq War":

> Defendants charged with unlawful reentry had the most extensive criminal histories. 90% had been previously arrested. Of those with a prior arrest, 50% had been arrested for violent or drug-related felonies. All of these crimes would have never happened, i.e. they were preventable, had we had a serious program of deportation of the illegal aliens already here and proper border security to prevent both entry and re-entry. In reviewing those numbers, note that the study sampled only about 21% of the incarcerated illegal aliens. To get the full extent of the collateral damage, we need to apply the average number of offenses across all 267,000 currently incarcerated illegal alien criminals. Doing so results in 1,288,619 crimes! Don't let the mainstream media and illegal alien advocates tell you that illegal immigration is a "victimless crime" and that they are here only to do the work Americans don't want to do. . . . The ones not caught and the new criminals crossing daily are committing more crime each and every day.[18]

Fortunately there are reputable studies that refute these inflated fig-ures and distorted logic. I will start with the National Research Coun-cil report mentioned in the previous section, released in the late 1990s by the Panel on the Demographic and Economic Impacts of Immi-gration. The chapter "Immigration and Crime in the United States" begins with a review of research from the nineteenth and early twen-tieth centuries:

> Aside from highly questionable writings associated with the eugenics movement, the research of this earlier era provided little evidence of a causal association between immigration and crime. . . .
>
> Where causality was seen to operate, its direction often was in the opposite direction expected. A report by the United States Immigration Commission found higher crime rates among the children of native-born parents and among children of immigrants than among immigrants themselves. . . . Such findings provided early support for the view that it was the acculturation of immigrants into American life that most notably increased their likelihood of involvement in crime.[19]

Moving on to review data from the latter part of the twentieth century, the authors "did not find consistent evidence in macro- or micro-level data that immigrants are much more likely than citizens of similar ages and gender to be involved in crime."[20] Regarding immigrants from Mexico specifically, the authors concluded that "Mexican immigrants are found in state prisons at an adjusted rate that is not strikingly differ-ent from U.S. citizens."[21]

Studies carried out in the first decade of the twenty-first century continue to bear out the National Research Council's conclusions. For example, as noted in a 2005 study commissioned by the Federal Reserve Bank of Chicago, "immigrants appear to be self-selected to have low criminal propensities."[22] "Getting Immigration Facts Straight," the SPLC report cited above, also cites many experts who refute the claim that immigrants are more likely to be criminals:

Ramiro Martinez Jr., a criminal justice professor at Florida Atlantic University who's spent years studying homicide statistics in U.S. border cities heavily populated by Mexican-born men and women, found the homicide rates were significantly lower for Latinos there than for other groups—even though the Latinos' poverty level was very high, and poverty and criminality are closely correlated statistically. Criminologist Andrew Karmen, in his 2006 book *New York Murder Mystery*, found the same trend in New York City, where the "disproportionately youthful, male and poor immigrants" of the last two decades "were surprisingly law abiding." Robert J. Sampson, chairman of Harvard's sociology department, reported in a 2005 article in *The American Journal of Health* that the rate of violence among Mexican Americans was significantly lower than among non-Latino white and black Americans. Remarkably, studies by sociologists Alejandro Portes and Rubén Rumbaut also show that second- and third-generation immigrants are significantly more criminal than their parents, suggesting that U.S. culture somehow eventually produces more, not less, criminality among its citizens.[23]

Interestingly, a study by the Pew Research Center published just a few weeks prior to this book going to production found that children of immigrants, rather than being criminally inclined as alleged by the xenophobes, are actually more educated than their peers and are less likely to live in poverty than the general population. The study also found that nearly 80 percent of Latinos and Latinas believed that "most people can get ahead if they're willing to work hard," whereas only 58 percent of the overall population felt that way.[24]

The ProCon.org article mentioned above also provides a sampling of expert studies on the correlation between crime rates and immigration. For example, William F. McDonald of the Georgetown University Law Center had this to say in his 2006 testimony before Congress:

The criminality of the first generation of immigrants (those who migrated as opposed to their children) is less than that of the native-born. There have been many studies in the United States and abroad that have addressed the question of the criminality of immigrants. . . .

There is little reason to believe that the findings would be substantially different for illegal immigrants assuming data were available that would allow us to make the necessary statistical controls for age, sex, economic status and immigrant status. Public fears about immigrant criminality have usually not been borne out by research.[25]

ProCon.org also cited a 2007 study by the American Immigration Law Foundation authored by Rubén G. Rumbaut and Walter A. Ewing:

Because many immigrants to the United States, especially Mexicans and Central Americans, are young men who arrive with very low levels of formal education, popular stereotypes tend to associate them with higher rates of crime and incarceration. . . .

However, data from the census and other sources show that for every ethnic group without exception, incarceration rates among young men are lowest for immigrants, even those who are the least educated. This holds true especially for the Mexicans, Salvadorans, and Guatemalans who make up the bulk of the undocumented population. The problem of crime in the United States is not "caused" or even aggravated by immigrants, regardless of their legal status.[26]

In 2008 the Public Policy Institute of California, based in the state with the largest percentage of immigrants, conducted a study that found no correlation between immigration and crime. Its findings are in stark contrast to media portrayals of Latino youth in California such as films like *American Me* and *Blood In, Blood Out.*

We find that the foreign-born, who make up about 35 percent of the adult population in California, constitute only about 17 percent of the adult prison population. Thus, immigrants are underrepresented in California prisons compared to their representation in the overall population. In fact, U.S.-born adult men are incarcerated at a rate over two-and-a-half times greater than that of foreign-born men. The difference only grows when we expand our investigation. When we consider all institutional-ization (not only prisons but also jails, halfway houses, and the like) and focus on the population that is most likely to be in institutions because of criminal activity (men ages 18–40), we find that, in California, U.S.-born men have an institutionalization rate that is 10 times higher than that of foreign-born men (4.2% vs. 0.42%). And when we compare foreign-born men to U.S.-born men with similar age and education levels, these differ-ences become even greater.[27]

In signing the tough anti-immigrant legislation SB 1070 in 2010, Ari-zona governor Jan Brewer stated that the bill's purpose was to reduce crime. A *Daily Beast* reporter took issue with the governor's logic and cited yet another study on the low criminality of immigrants:

A new study by sociologist Tim Wadsworth of the University of Colorado at Boulder carefully evaluates the various factors behind the statistics that show a massive drop in crime during the 1990s at a time when immigra-tion rose dramatically. In a peer-reviewed paper appearing in the June 2010 issue of *Social Science Quarterly,* Wadsworth argues not only that "cities with the largest increases in immigration between 1990 and 2000 experienced the largest decreases in homicide and robbery," which we knew, but that after considering all the other explanations, rising immi-gration "was partially responsible."

To deny that reality and ignore its implications is likely to make life more dangerous all over America, diverting resources away from the fight against violent crime and breaking down the hard-won trust between cops and the communities where they work. Several police chiefs tried to make exactly this point Wednesday on a visit to Washington to talk about the Arizona law, due to take effect in July, and the bad precedent it sets. "This is not a law that increases public safety. This is a bill that makes it much harder for us to do our jobs," said Los Angeles Police Chief Charlie Beck. "Crime will go up if this becomes law in Arizona or in any other state."[28]

With respect to the claim of a nexus between illegal immigration and terrorism, a report sponsored by the Migration Policy Institute observes that

> terrorism experts have targeted controlling illegal immigration as a top priority, and many opponents of immigration have jumped on the opportunity to promote their policy and political objectives on this issue.
>
> Yet irregular immigrants and terrorists are fundamentally different. The former seek work and/or the opportunity to reunify with their families. The latter follow the dictates of religious firebrands who apparently seek to promote religious and political goals at home through terrorist acts there and abroad. Recruiting terrorists from among irregular immigrants or "disguising" terrorists as irregular immigrants is certainly a possibility, but so far neither seems to be a preferred option. . . .
>
> [M]ost would-be terrorists are likely to continue to enter through a legal port of entry. Even the best visa and border inspection systems cannot prevent such entries because the intelligence on which a state's frontline officials make decisions about whom to allow in will never be foolproof. This is not an "immigration" issue; it is an issue of trying to make error-free decisions about the billions of international travelers who cross borders each year.[29]

Simply put, despite the rhetoric, increases in immigration do not correlate with increases in crime rates, much less cause them. In fact, first-generation immigrants have been shown to exhibit lower criminal propensity rates than native-born Americans, and it is only their children, the second and third generations, raised in the Americanized culture, who begin to exhibit signs of higher criminal propensities. The anti-immigrant lobby is simply wrong.

The Alleged Economic Drain on the Nation's Economy

Throughout this country's history, especially during times of war, perceived political unrest, or economic downturn, policy makers have blamed undocumented immigrants for America's problems. The tendency continues to this day. From every major media outlet and even in the White House, we hear that undocumented immigration is significantly harming the nation's economy. But despite the frequency and repetitiveness of assertions that undocumented immigrants are a drain on our economy, depress wages, and take jobs away from citizens, these statements are simply not supported by the evidence.

Indeed, economic analysts as well as domestic business community mainstays have long advocated for less restrictive immigration policies.[30] As a leading immigration scholar observed, "The U.S. immigration laws must be fundamentally revised to make them and their enforcement more consistent with the economic needs of the nation."[31] As another observer noted,

> In defiance of economic logic, U.S. lawmakers formulate immigration policies to regulate the entry of foreign workers into the country that are largely unrelated to the economic policies they formulate to regulate international commerce. Perpetuating the status quo by pouring ever larger amounts of money into the enforcement of immigration policies that are in conflict with economic reality will do nothing to address the underlying problem.[32]

Bill Gates, founder of Microsoft, repeatedly complained that strict immigration policies impeded the ability of businesses to hire skilled workers.[33] Regarding unskilled workers, an American Farm Bureau Federation study notes that "if agriculture's access to migrant labor were cut off, as much as $5-to-9 billion in annual production of . . . commodities . . . would be lost in the short term. Over the longer term, this annual loss would increase to $6.5-to-12 billion as the shock worked its way through the sector."[34] John Kenneth Galbraith's thoughts on undocumented workers are as relevant now as they were almost thirty-five years ago:

> Were all the illegals in the United States suddenly to return home, the effect on the American economy would . . . be little less than disastrous. A large amount of useful, if often tedious, work . . . would go unperformed.

Fruits and vegetables in Florida, Texas, and California would go unhar-vested. Food prices would rise spectacularly. Mexicans wish to come to the United States; they are wanted; they add visibly to our well-being. . . . Without them, the American economy would suffer.[35]

This section will examine the three main ways undocumented immigra-tion is said to affect the economy: (1) the overall fiscal impact, that is, cost versus benefits, GDP, and so forth; (2) effect on domestic wages; and (3) effect on domestic jobs. Each of the anti-immigrant economic-based arguments is addressed, and dispelled, in turn, using respected economic empirical studies and not mere rhetoric. Indeed, study after study has demonstrated that undocumented immigration is vital to domestic business interests and provides an overall benefit to our nation's economic well-being.

The Fiscal Benefits versus the Costs of Undocumented Immigrants

Perhaps the most useful way to start this section is to discuss the meth-odology used by those who claim that illegal immigration constitutes a grave detriment to our economy. A good example is this calculation from a 2007 Heritage Foundation study:

> Receiving, on average, at least $22,449 more in benefits than they pay in taxes each year, low-skill households impose substantial long-term costs on the U.S. taxpayer. Assuming an average 50-year adult life span for heads of household, the average lifetime costs to the taxpayer will be $1.1 million for each low-skill household.

This is relevant to our discussion of immigration policy because the report makes clear that "changes in immigration law that would signifi-cantly increase the inflow of low-skill workers and families will increase future government spending dramatically."[36]

A major flaw of the Heritage Foundation study is that it does not pay adequate attention to the economic benefit of undocumented immigrants, and even more so, the benefits of their children, once they have been educated and are working and paying taxes. Once immigrants are assimilated into the economy and become members of the community, they provide real gains that we will see put back into the American economy.[37] This will be a permanent and continuing contribution, whereas the potential burden an immigrant family would place on the overall public, in the event they are receiving need-based services, presumably would be temporary and later offset by their contributions via future taxable income. Moreover, many immigrants would not be eligible for public benefit services for at least five years after they obtain their legal permanent resident status. Even the critical Heritage Foundation studies show that whether a family dependent on the public welfare system is native-born or not, the detriment to the economy is the same. Finally, a critical flaw of the study is that it fails to distinguish between undocumented and documented immigration. Therefore, its conclusions are largely inapplicable to the undocumented immigration debate.

Following its highly criticized previous studies on the fiscal impact of undocumented immigration, just a few weeks before the publication date of this book, the Heritage Foundation published its 2013 study on the issue by yet again using the same author, Robert Rector, joined this time by Jason Richwine. This study claims that a comprehensive immigration reform plan that provides a form of legalization for the undocumented will cost the country over $54 billion. Not surprisingly, the Rector and Richwine report was immediately and rightfully discredited. Not only is the credibility of the study's co-author Richwine made questionable in light of his eugenics-like dissertation, which argues that immigrants have substantially lower IQs than Whites,[38] but the economic premise of the 2013 report in itself appears fatally flawed. As the CATO Institute, U.S. Senator Marco Rubio, and Fox News Commentator Juan Willams have observed, the 2013 report focuses soley on costs of the undocumented, without considering dynamic growth associated with immigration, or economic benefits created by the undocumented.[39] Thus, the 2013 Heritage Foundation study is cursed with being plagued with potentially racist implications, and once again illegitimate as a result of being one-sided, and thus economically unsound.

Thus, the argument that low-skilled immigrants will be a larger public charge would be true only if one does not take into account the more than offsetting benefits immigrants provide to our economy. Moreover, the Heritage Foundation studies presuppose that the majority of the incoming immigrants are low-skilled, but if this is true, it is true in the short run at best. By looking at the overall economic picture, as the other studies examined here will do, and by drafting a policy to prioritize selection of incoming immigrants based on demand, policy makers would find immigration creates positive impacts even in the short term for the U.S. economy.

The Heritage Foundation's conclusions are challenged by virtually all credible studies on the fiscal effects of undocumented immigration. The following are excerpts of the leading studies examining the fiscal impact of undocumented immigration on the nation's economy.

1998 National Research Council Report

The National Research Council report refutes the claim that undocumented immigrants have an overall negative impact on the economy. In fact, the report argues, undocumented immigrants provide

> a net positive fiscal impact with immigrants and their concurrent descendants paying nearly $51 billion [in 1994–1995 dollars] more in taxes than they generate in costs. . . . Particularly important were transfers from immigrants and their descendants of about $28 billion to the rest of the nation through the Social Security system (OASDHI), reflecting the young age distribution of this group. . . .
>
> In per capita terms, immigrants and their concurrent descendants contributed about $700 more in payroll taxes than they received in OASDHI benefits each year, whereas the balance of the population just broke even. For the remainder of the federal budget, immigrants and their concurrent descendants paid $500 or $600 more in taxes than they cost in benefits, and in total they had a positive federal fiscal impact of about $1,260 [per person], exceeding their net cost at the state and local levels.[40]

With respect to overall economic impact, the NRC report concludes,

Our calculations indicate that definition of the study population is critical to the outcome. If limited to immigrants themselves, the overall fiscal
impact is $1,400 (taxes paid less costs generated) per immigrant. If lim-
ited to immigrants plus their U.S.-born children under the age of 20, cor-
responding to the immigrant household formulation, the average fiscal
impact is about -$600 per immigrant (or -$400 per immigrant and young
child). If extended to all descendants of living immigrants, the average
fiscal impact is $1,000 expressed per immigrant, or $600 expressed per
immigrant and descendants. Therefore, the most widely used method
based on the immigrant household is the only one that returns a negative
value.[41]

2001 Cato Institute Congressional Testimony

The Cato Institute's positions on a host of issues would appropriately be
construed as either libertarian or conservative. For instance, on matters
such as the Second Amendment to the Constitution, the Cato Institute
takes a conservative approach that differs with the views of the author of
this book. Politics aside, however, the Cato Institute has commissioned
leading scholars to issue reports and provide congressional testimony
that are in substantive agreement with the NRC report and the other
major studies on immigration analyzed here.

In his April 2001 testimony before the Senate Subcommittee on
Immigration, Stephen Moore, Senior Fellow in Economics at the Cato
Institute, opened his remarks by noting that a

consensus seems to have emerged . . . that immigrants are—as they have
been throughout most of our history—beneficial to our economy and
assets to our society in other ways as well. This favorable attitude. . . .
reflects the growing consensus within the economics profession that
immigrants are on balance economic assets, not liabilities. To be sure,

economists still argue about the size of the benefit of immigration to the U.S. economy, but almost all of the best research indicates that the direction of the impact is on balance positive.[42]

Moore provides a good summary of the various fears about the effects of immigration:

> Many advocates of a lower level of immigration, or even in some extreme cases, a moratorium on immigration, argued that continued high levels of immigration would lead to such economic problems as (1) increased unemployment for native born workers; (2) higher poverty rates of native born Americans; (3) lower incomes for American workers; (4) increased economic problems for minority workers; (5) a huge surge in welfare dependency; and (6) lower overall rates of economic growth.
>
> But it didn't happen. None of these claims have been evidenced in the U.S. economy. . . . And here there is little debate. High levels of immigration have corresponded with improvement in each of these areas, not with the problems getting worse.[43]

Moore noted that his own research reached conclusions similar to those of the NRC report, which he called "the most comprehensive study ever conducted on immigration," and which "found that immigrants inflate the incomes of U.S. born workers by at least $10 billion each year."[44]

Moore also mentioned the impacts on state and local economies:

> Immigrants pay their own way when it comes to services used and taxes paid. Immigrants use many government services—particularly at the state and local levels—but they also pay a lot in taxes. Conservatively estimated, in 1998 immigrant households paid an estimated $133 billion in direct taxes to federal, state and local governments. Adding the tax receipts paid by immigrant businesses brings the total annual tax contributions of immigrants to about $162 billion for 1998. In any given year, immigrants may use more in services than they pay in taxes, but over their lifetimes, immigrants

are a fiscal bargain to native taxpayers. As their earnings rise over time, immigrant taxes exceed the benefits received.[45]

Moore also concluded that overall, immigrants are "huge net contributors to the Social Security and Medicare programs" and "a major source of new jobs and vitality in the American economy."[46] Moore ended his testimony with the following observation:

> It is in America's economic self-interest—and in the interests of immigrants themselves—that we keep the golden gates open to newcomers from every region of the world. The net gains to U.S. workers and retirees are in the trillions of dollars. Given the coming retirement of some 75 million baby boomers, we need the young and energetic immigrants now more than ever before.[47]

2008 Centre of Policy Studies Report

In 2008 the Centre of Policy Studies released a report entitled "Reducing Illegal Migrants in the U.S.: A Dynamic CGE Analysis," authored by two of its own researchers, Peter B. Dixon and Maureen T. Rimmer, and by Martin Johnson of the U.S. Department of Commerce. The authors modeled the probable results of two types of immigration policies: supply-restricting and demand-restricting. An approach that reduces the supply of undocumented immigrants basically increases the costs to undocumented immigrants by, among other things, increasing border security, increasing deportation, and causing smugglers to charge higher fees. Such a policy, according to this study, "causes a long-run reduction in United States employment," a roughly equivalent "long-run reduction in the capital stock of the U.S.," and a "long-run reduction in GDP."[48] When the authors "simulate the effects of restricting the supply of illegal workers, we find that job numbers fall relatively sharply in those industries in which there is a significant replacement of low-productivity illegal workers with higher-productivity legal workers."[49] In contrast, the effects on domestic workers of a supply-reducing policy would be negligible: "in the absence of supply shocks to the legal workforce, wage adjustments ensure that the policy of restricting foreign-illegal immigration can have no more than minor effects on long-run employment of legal U.S. residents."[50]

In contrast, demand-reducing policies, such as taxing employers of undocumented immigrants, would overall be less damaging than supply-reducing policies: "Supply-restricting programs allow the foreign-illegal employees who remain in the U.S. to capture the increase in cost as an increase in their wage rate. Demand-contracting programs, implemented by taxes and fines, transfer all of the cost increase (and more) to the U.S. Treasury."[51] In the case of demand-reducing programs through increases in "criminal prosecutions, the extra costs are likely to be a dissipation of real resources through the use of lawyers, accountants and other professionals involved in defending charges and mitigating their effects."[52]

The study concludes that the only reform option that provides an arguable net benefit to this country is a policy that increases taxes on domestic employers, which would benefit the U.S. Treasury, which in turn could theoretically benefit U.S. residents through improved programs sponsored by the federal government. For some reason, this report's only option benefiting this country does not find any policy that could be undertaken to benefit U.S. households. Perhaps consequently, this study has not garnered as much attention or favor as the Cato Institute study I will discuss next, though it was conducted by the same people.

2009 Cato Institute Report

In August 2009 the Cato Institute issued its report "Restriction or Legalization? Measuring the Economic Benefits of Immigration Reform," written by Peter Dixon and Maureen Rimmer, who analyzed the projected effects of seven distinct immigration policy scenarios. The report's methodology and major findings are described in the executive summary:

Proposed policy responses range from more restrictive border and workplace enforcement to legalization of workers who are already here and the admission of new workers through a temporary visa program. . . .

This study uses the U.S. Applied General Equilibrium model that has been developed for the U.S. International Trade Commission and other U.S. government agencies to estimate the welfare impact of seven different scenarios, which include increased enforcement at the border and in the workplace, and several different legalization options, including a visa program that allows more low-skilled workers to enter the U.S. workforce legally.

For each scenario, the USAGE model weighs the impact on such factors as public revenues and expenditures, the occupational mix and total employment of U.S. workers, the amount of capital owned by U.S. households, and price levels for imports and exports. This study finds that increased enforcement and reduced low-skilled immigration have a significant negative impact on the income of U.S. households. Modest savings in public expenditures would be more than offset by losses in economic output and job opportunities for more-skilled American workers. A policy that reduces the number of low-skilled immigrant workers by 28.6 percent compared to projected levels would reduce U.S. household welfare by about 0.5 percent, or $80 billion.

In contrast, legalization of low-skilled immigrant workers would yield significant income gains for American workers and households. Legalization would eliminate smugglers' fees and other costs faced by illegal immigrants. It would also allow immigrants to have higher productivity and create more openings for Americans in higher skilled occupations. The positive impact for U.S. households of legalization under an optimal visa tax would be 1.27 percent of GDP or $180 billion.[53]

The seven scenarios include two that are more restrictive and five that are more liberal:

In the first two simulations, the policies restrict illegal immigration. In Simulation 1, the restrictive policy is tighter border enforcement; in Simulation 2, it is tighter internal enforcement. In the other five simulations, we consider policies in which illegal immigration is largely replaced by programs of entry visas. Under such programs, employers in the United States would be able to offer jobs on a temporary basis to people outside the country. Such a policy change would largely eliminate smugglers' fees and other costs of illegal entry, thereby inducing an increase in the supply of what we will now refer to as guest workers.[54]

Results of the more restrictive policies were markedly negative:

A major finding of the study is that the program of tighter border enforcement, Simulation 1, strongly reduces the welfare of U.S. households. A principal effect is that it raises the wage rate of the illegal immigrants who remain in the United States, in effect transferring income from legal residents of the United States to illegal immigrants. Even more importantly, restricting the inflow of illegal immigrants biases the occupational mix of employment for U.S. workers toward low-paying, low-skilled jobs as those jobs become relatively more attractive and available compared with higher-paying occupations. This eventually reduces the overall productivity of U.S. workers and consequently their average real wage rate.

Tighter internal enforcement, Simulation 2, has negative effects similar in magnitude to that of Simulation 1. Rather than the scarcity value of illegal immigrants being realized as an increase in illegal wage rates, it is dissipated in prosecution mitigating activities by employers, including the hiring of lawyers, accountants, and other professionals. In the language of economics, the scarcity value of illegal immigrants is translated into a dead-weight loss.

In Simulation 1, increased border security moves the supply curve for illegal immigrants sufficiently inwards to reduce their employment in the United States in 2019 by 28.6 percent, from 12.4 million in the business-as-usual run to 8.8 million in the policy run. This reduces the welfare of U.S. households by the equivalent of 0.55 percent of the gross national product, or $80 billion in today's economy. The internal enforcement scenario, Simulation 2, is scaled to have a similar effect on illegal employment as that in Simulation 1.[55]

Conversely, the more liberal scenarios consistently yielded gains:

> Legalization produces a strong welfare gain for U.S. households. With legalization, the supply of immigrants (now guest workers) increases and their average wage falls. At the same time, the additional inflow of guest workers has a favorable effect on the occupational mix and average real wage rate of U.S. workers. Allowing low-skilled workers to enter the country legally would boost the welfare of U.S. households by 0.57 percent of GNP.[56]

The differences in outcome between Simulation 1 and Simulation 7 are striking: "Our simulations show that the difference between the long-run welfare effects for U.S. households of the worst and best policies that we considered is about $260 billion a year in current dollars. This is the welfare gap between the tighter-border-enforcement policy in Simulation 1 (a welfare loss of 0.55 percent) and the liberalized policy with an optimal visa charge in Simulation 7 (a welfare gain of 1.27 percent)."[57] Per household, these amounts may be small, but over a period of time, if the projections are correct, the gains could cumulatively result in a substantial increase in the quality of living for many U.S. households.

2009 Migration Policy Institute Report

In "The Economics and Policy of Illegal Immigration in the United States," a 2009 report for the Migration Policy Institute, the economist Gordon Hanson stressed the benefits to U.S. employers of the work performed by undocumented immigrants:

> Since 2001, policy makers have poured huge resources onto securing U.S. borders, ports, and airports; and since 2006, a growing range of policies has targeted unauthorized immigrants. . . . [But] illegal immigration has been hugely beneficial to many U.S. employers, often providing benefits that the current legal immigration system does not. . . .

Not only do unauthorized immigrants provide an important source of low-skilled labor, they also respond to market conditions in ways that legal immigration presently cannot, making them particularly appealing to U.S. employers.[58]

Like the authors of the Cato Institute report, Hanson also recommends a policy of enhancing the legal entry of low-skilled workers: "A more constructive immigration policy would aim to generate maximum productivity gains to the U.S. economy while limiting the fiscal cost and keeping enforcement spending contained. Effectively, this means converting existing inflows of illegal immigrants into legal flows."[59]

2010 Immigration Policy Center Report

In January 2010 the Immigration Policy Center, a pro-immigrant think tank that is well regarded in immigration circles, issued a report authored by the UCLA professor Raúl Hinojosa-Ojeda. "Raising the Floor for American Workers: The Economic Benefits of Comprehensive Immigration Reform" reached conclusions similar to the reports discussed above:

Comprehensive immigration reform that legalizes currently unauthorized immigrants and creates flexible legal limits on future immigration in the context of full labor rights would help American workers and the U.S. economy. Unlike the current enforcement-only strategy, comprehensive reform would raise the "wage floor" for the entire U.S. economy—to the benefit of both immigrant and native-born workers.

The historical experience of legalization under the 1986 Immigration Reform and Control Act, or IRCA indicates that comprehensive immigration reform would raise wages, increase consumption, create jobs, and generate additional tax revenue. Even though IRCA was implemented during an economic recession characterized by high unemployment, it still helped raise wages and spurred increases in educational, home, and small-business investments by newly legalized immigrants. Taking the experience of IRCA as a starting point, we estimate that comprehensive immigration reform would yield at least $1.5 trillion in cumulative U.S. gross domestic product over 10 years.[60]

Three distinct scenarios are considered: a temporary worker program and mass deportation are compared to what the report describes as "comprehensive reform":

> This report uses a computable general equilibrium model to estimate the economic ramifications of three different scenarios: (1) comprehensive immigration reform that creates a pathway to legal status for unauthorized immigrants in the United States and establishes flexible limits on permanent and temporary immigration that respond to changes in U.S. labor demand in the future; (2) a program for temporary workers only that does not include a pathway to permanent status or more flexible legal limits on permanent immigration in the future; and (3) mass deportation to expel all unauthorized immigrants and effectively seal the U.S.-Mexico border.[61]

The first scenario, comprehensive immigration reform, "generates an increase in U.S. GDP of at least 0.84 percent. Summed over 10 years, this amounts to a cumulative $1.5 trillion in additional GDP. It also boosts wages for both native-born and newly legalized immigrant workers."[62]

In contrast, the second scenario, a temporary worker program, would generate a smaller increase in GDP of 0.44 percent, which "amounts to $792 billion of cumulative GDP over 10 years."[63] Moreover, such a program would have detrimental effects on wages and would actually increase levels of immigration:

> Immigrant workers in this scenario have limited labor rights, which drives down wages and productivity for all workers in industries where large numbers of immigrants are employed. This legal immigration would respond to changes in U.S. labor demand, but at relatively low wages and without the build up of human capital and labor productivity that occurs

over time among legalized workers. As a result, future levels of immigration are actually higher under this scenario than under comprehensive immigration reform since more workers are needed to produce the same level of output under these low-wage, low-productivity conditions.[64]

The third scenario considered in the report, mass deportation, "reduces U.S. GDP by 1.46 percent. This amounts to $2.6 trillion in cumulative lost GDP over 10 years, not including the actual cost of deportation. Wages would rise for less-skilled native-born workers, but would diminish for higher-skilled natives, and would lead to widespread job loss."[65] The author also notes that "while this [mass deportation] scenario estimates the broader economic impact of mass deportation, it does not take into account the actual cost of mass deportation. The Center for American Progress has pegged this cost at somewhere between $206 billion and $230 billion over five years.[66]

The report also addressed the unintended consequences of this country's current border policies:

> Enforcement-only border policies have not stopped or even slowed the pace of unauthorized immigration, but they have distorted the migration process in ways that produce unintended consequences that are detrimental to the U.S. economy, American workers, and unauthorized immigrants themselves, including: making the southwestern border more lethal; . . . creating new opportunities for people smugglers; . . . breaking circular migration and promoting permanent settlement in the United States; . . . [and] depressing low-wage labor markets.[67]

As the author succinctly puts it, "'Enforcement Only' is costly, ineffective, and counterproductive."[68]

2011 Dixon and Rimmer Report

In 2011 an article in the journal *Contemporary Economic Policy* was published by Peter B. Dixon, Maureen T. Rimmer, and Martin Johnson, the coauthors of the 2008 Centre of Policy Studies report discussed above and (in the case of Dixon and Rimmer) the coauthors of the 2009 Cato Institute report. In the article, "Economy-Wide Effects of Reducing Illegal Immigrants in U.S. Employment," the authors again apply the USAGE model, but they concentrate on three rather than seven scenarios: one supply-restricting approach ("tighter border security"), and two demand-restricting approaches ("taxes on employers; and vigorous prosecution of employers").[69]

The supply-restricting approach—that is, tighter border security— "causes a long-run . . . reduction in jobs of 2.2%, . . . mainly reflect[ing] the reduction of 3.55 million in the number of illegal jobs," but it also "leads to a long-run reduction in the welfare of legal residents."[70] The authors favor a policy of taxes and fines on employers, which of course mean extra costs for employers, but "these extra costs . . . are a transfer to the U.S. Treasury which is then able to improve the welfare of legal residents through tax cuts or increased public spending," whereas the costs of criminally prosecuting employers "are likely to be a dissipation of real resources through the use of lawyers and other professionals involved in defending charges and mitigating their effects."[71] Overall, however, this study is not as useful as some of the others examined in this section; it analyzes only two types of policies: tighter border security and increased domestic employer sanctions, rather than legislating pathways to legalization.

Thus, with the exception of highly criticized reports published by the Heritage Foundation, the overwhelming majority of the studies to examine the issue of the fiscal impact of documented immigration conclude that immigration has a net positive impact on the nation's overall well-being and provides overall gains to domestic households. In terms of solutions to undocumented immigration, these studies agree that the worst alternative would be policies focused on strict border enforcement that have the effect of reducing immigration. Accordingly, these studies find that policies that provide a form of legalization of this workforce are far more beneficial to the domestic economy, domestic worker wages, and U.S. households.

Undocumented Immigration's Effects on Domestic Wages

Related to the first anti-immigrant economic-based argument—that undocumented immigrants hurt our economy—the second argument is that the influx of undocumented workers has a negative effect on wages of domestic workers. The Southern Poverty Law Center report provides several examples of such arguments put forth by media figures: Lou Dobbs, for example, asserted on his show "that the 'most authoritative' study showed that legal and illegal immigration was depressing native wages by $200 billion a year. California nativist activist Joe Guzzardi has claimed that wages remain 'stagnant' because of illegal immigrants."[72] According to these arguments, legalizing several million undocumented workers and allowing hundreds of thousands of new workers to enter legally each year will ultimately lower wages for average domestic workers.

In a 2008 working paper for the National Bureau of Economic Research, the economists George J. Borjas, Jeffrey Grogger, and Gordon H. Hanson describe the methodology that leads them to conclude that "immigration appears likely to lower the wages of those native workers most affected by immigration-induced supply shifts."[73] However, most economists have found that domestic workers are not easily replaced by undocumented immigrants, due to a number of reasons, including language barriers, logistics, education, and training. In more traditional economic parlance, domestic workers are imperfect substitutes for undocumented workers. While they do find a "small wage loss" among those domestic workers who have dropped out of high school, the wages of all other domestic workers benefit from immigrant workers.

Among those who argue that undocumented and domestic workers are imperfect substitutes are the economists Gianmarco Ottaviano and Giovanni Peri. In a 2005 working paper for the National Bureau of Economic Research (NBER), they conclude that,

> whereas it is hard to deny that in any reasonable model, the relative increase of low skilled workers will cause a decrease in their relative wage,

this study is interested primarily in determining the overall (average) effect of immigration, aggregating across groups of U.S.-born workers. It turns out both empirically and theoretically that immigration, as we have known it during the nineties, had a sizeable beneficial effect on the wages of U.S.-born workers. For a flow of migrants that increases total employment by 10% and a skill distribution that mirrors the one observed in the nineties, U.S.-born workers experience a 3–4 percentage point increase in their wages. This results because U.S. and foreign-born workers are not perfectly substitutable, even when they have similar observable skills. Workers born, raised and partly educated in foreign environments are not identical to workers born and raised in the U.S.[74]

The same authors expanded on their conclusions in another NBER report published the following year:

The main message of this paper is that only within a model that specifies the interactions between workers of different skills and between labor and physical capital (in a production function) can we derive marginal productivity, labor demands and analyze the effects of immigration on the wages of different types of workers. The existing literature on immigration has paid much attention to the estimates of the partial effect of immigrants on wages of U.S.-born workers with similar skills. Those estimates are *partial* in that they assume a constant supply of all other groups and of physical capital and therefore are not informative of the actual overall effects of immigration on wages. In taking the general equilibrium approach instead, one realizes that the substitutability between U.S.- and foreign-born workers with similar schooling and experience, as well as the investment response to changes in the supply of skills are important parameters in evaluating the short and long run effects of immigration on wages. We therefore carefully tackle the tasks of estimating the elasticity of substitution between U.S.- and foreign-born workers within education-experience and gender cells and we account for physical capital adjustment in the short and long run. We find robust evidence that U.S.- and foreign-born workers are not perfect substitutes within an education-experience-gender group. This fact, and the yearly adjustment of capital to immigration, imply that average wages of natives benefit from immigration, even in the short run. These average gains are, in the short and long run, distributed as a small wage loss to the group of high school dropouts and wage gains for all the other groups of U.S. natives. The group suffering the biggest loss in wages is the contingent of previous immigrants, who compete with new immigrants for similar jobs and occupations. Finally, our model implies that it is hard to claim that immigration has been a significant determinant in the deterioration of the wage distribution of U.S.-born workers during the period 1990–2004.[75]

A 2007 report from the President's Council of Economic Advisers also agreed that "immigrants tend to complement (not substitute for) natives, raising natives' productivity and income," and that "immigration has a positive effect on the American economy as a whole and on the income of native-born American workers":

Fully 90% of US native-born workers are estimated to have gained from immigration. Multiplying the average percentage gains by the total wages of US natives suggests that annual wage gains from immigration are between $30 billion and $80 billion. . . .

[N]atives benefit from immigration because the complementarities associated with immigrants outweigh any losses from added labor market competition. . . . The number of natives with less than a high school degree has declined over time, which is one reason less-skilled immigrants have been drawn into the US labor force to fill relatively low-paying jobs. Even so, . . . one might expect the remaining least-skilled natives to face labor market competition from immigrants. Evidence on this issue is mixed. Studies often find small negative effects of immigration on the wages of low-skilled natives, and even the comparatively large estimate reported in Borjas (2003) is under 10% for immigration over a 20 year period. The difficulties faced by high school dropouts are a serious policy concern, but it is safe to conclude that immigration is not a central cause of those difficulties, nor is reducing immigration a well-targeted way to help these low-wage natives.[76]

Giovanni Peri also coauthored, with Chad Sparber, a 2008 discussion paper for the Centre for Research and Analysis of Migration entitled "Task Specialization, Immigration, and Wages." Again the study finds only small-scale reduction in wages for some workers, because "native and foreign-born workers with little formal education are imperfect substitutes in production."[77]

> Large inflows of less-educated immigrants would reduce wages paid to comparably-educated native-born workers if the two groups are perfectly substitutable in production. In a simple model exploiting comparative advantage, however, we show that if less-educated foreign and native-born workers specialize in performing different tasks, immigration will cause natives to reallocate their task supply, thereby reducing downward wage pressure . . . foreign-born workers specialize in occupations that require manual and physical labor skills while natives pursue jobs more intensive in communication and language tasks. Immigration induces natives to specialize accordingly. Simulations show that this increased specialization might explain why economic analyses commonly find only modest wage and employment consequences of immigration for less-educated native-born workers across U.S. states. This is especially true in states with large immigration flows.[78]

The authors conclude that "productivity gains from specialization, coupled with the high compensation paid to communication skills, together imply that foreign-born workers do not create large adverse consequences for wages paid to less-educated natives."[79]

In another report for the Centre for Research and Analysis of Migration the following year, the economist David Card surveyed the larger picture of income inequality in the United States over the last several decades and concluded that the growing gap between higher-wage and lower-wage workers cannot be blamed on immigration: "the average impacts of recent immigrant inflows on the relative wages of U.S. natives are small . . . immigration accounts for a small share (5%) of the increase in U.S. wage inequality between 1980 and 2000."[80] Card also reaffirmed the conclusion that "within broad education classes, immigrant and native workers appear to be imperfect substitutes, with a large but finite elasticity of substitution. As first pointed out by Ottaviano and Peri (2006), if immigrants and natives in the same skill category are imperfect substitutes, the competitive effects of additional immigrant inflows are concentrated among immigrants themselves, lessening the impacts on natives.[81]

In a 2010 New Policy Institute report titled "The Impact of Immigration and Immigration Reform on the Wages of American Workers," the economists Robert Shapiro and Jiwon Vellucci attempt to counter what they call the "alarming amounts of misinformation . . . being presented as facts."[82] While they acknowledge that the wages of some low-skilled workers are negatively affected, the larger picture is more positive: "A careful review shows that high levels of immigration have not slowed overall wage gains by average, native-born American workers. Most studies suggest that recent waves of new immigrants are associated with increases in the average wage of native-born Americans in the short-run and with even larger increases in the long term as capital investment rises to take account of the larger number of workers."[83]

> The distribution of immigrants' education and skills, compared to those of native-born Americans, produces adverse effects on the incomes of low-skilled Americans, positive effects on the incomes of skilled Americans, and overall gains in the national income and Gross Domestic Product (GDP). . . .
>
> . . . An influx of new, low-skilled workers also can ultimately produce net overall gains for American workers, from a number of sources. To begin, the wage gains of the highly-skilled workers are usually greater than the wage losses of the unskilled native workers, producing net benefits. Furthermore, the influx expands the labor force and increases total output, in part because many immigrants fill jobs that native-born Americans would not fill, increasing national income.[84]

The authors also discuss how immigration reform affects wages: "legal changes which enable undocumented immigrants to secure legal status, and thus qualify for minimum wage, would increase the overall gains to GDP or national income, and generate positive wage effects for low-skilled native-Americans."[85]

> The largest effects [of immigration reform] are felt by those immigrants themselves: Following the 1986 immigration reform, wages increased by between 6 percent and 15 percent for previously-undocumented male immigrants and by 21 percent for previously undocumented female immigrants. Immigration reforms also increased the wages of immigrants who had already obtained legal status. Finally, research confirms that immigration reforms led to modest increases in wages for native-born Americans.[86]

With but one exception, then, the studies examining the issue conclude that undocumented immigration increases the wages of domestic workers. The reason for this effect is that undocumented workers are not perfect substitutes for domestic workers and the jobs the undocumented take actually provide greater opportunities for the English-speaking native workers to obtain higher-paying jobs in those same industries.

The Effect of Undocumented Immigration on Domestic Jobs

The third major economic argument against undocumented immigrants is the claim that they take away domestic jobs. The rhetoric is by now familiar. Once again I turn to the report by the Southern Poverty Law Center for a sampling of the rhetoric:

> The allegation that illegal immigrants are causing native unemployment is pervasive in the nativist movement. Terry Anderson, a black Los Angeles radio host and hard-line anti-immigration activist, for instance, told "Lou Dobbs Tonight" on Oct. 23, 2003, that legal and illegal immigration was "killing the [native-born] work force." Texas nativist leader

Debbie Rawlins said in 2006 that "Hispanics" were "taking our jobs, our homes." The far-right California Coalition for Immigration Reform has a billboard on the California-Arizona border that reads, "Demand Illegal Aliens Be Deported. The Job You Save May Be Your Own."[87]

Those who insist that immigrants take away jobs have been repeating the assertion for so long and with so little challenge that their claim is accepted as fact even without any evidence to support it. An examination of actual data reveals a much different picture.

In 2006, for example, a report from the Pew Hispanic Center found no clear or constant pattern of negative employment effects for domestic workers as a result of immigration. The report's author, the economist Rakesh Kochhar, reached the following conclusions:

> The employment prospects for native-born workers do not appear to be related to the growth of the foreign-born population. . . .
>
> . . . Regardless of the indicator used, when the employment outcome of the native-born population was measured against the percent change of the foreign-born population in each state, no constant pattern emerged. . . .
>
> . . . The size of the foreign-born workforce in a state appears to have no relationship to the employment prospects for native-born workers.
>
> The analysis also focused on two particular segments of the workforce that are entry points for a majority of foreign-born workers: workers with a high school education or less and workers ages 25 to 44. Despite the relative concentration of foreign-born workers in these segments, it appears to have had no discernible impact on the employment of less-educated and relatively young native-born workers.[88]

A 2009 report by the Immigration Policy Center is worth quoting at length:

> Some commentators argue that undocumented immigrants, who tend to have low levels of formal education and to work in less-skilled

occupations, are "taking" large numbers of jobs that might otherwise be filled by African American workers. . . . However, data from the U.S. Census Bureau reveals that this is not the case. In fact, there is little apparent relationship between recent immigration and unemployment rates among African Americans, or any other native-born racial/ethnic group, at the state or metropolitan level.

- States and metropolitan areas with the highest shares of recent immigrants in the labor force do not necessarily have the highest unemployment rates among native-born blacks, whites, Hispanics, or Asians. Nor do locales with the highest rates of unemployment among native-born blacks, whites, Hispanics, or Asians necessarily have the highest shares of recent immigrants in the labor force. . . .
- In the 10 states with the highest shares of recent immigrants in the labor force, the average unemployment rate for native-born blacks is about four percentage points less than in the ten states with the lowest shares of recent immigrants. . . .
- In the ten metropolitan areas with the highest shares of recent immigrants in the labor force, the unemployment rate for native-born blacks is about 1.5 percentage points less than in the 10 metropolitan areas with the lowest share of recent immigrants. . . .

The absence of any significant statistical correlation between recent immigration and unemployment rates among different native-born racial groups points to deeper, structural causes for unemployment among native-born, such as levels of educational attainment and work skills.[89]

In a 2010 article for the Federal Reserve Bank of San Francisco, Giovanni Peri provides a useful summary of previous work that he and Chad Sparber have carried out on the economic impact of immigration. Once again these studies refute the claim that immigrants take jobs away from domestic workers: "Consistent with previous research, the analysis finds no significant effect of immigration on net job growth for U.S.-born workers. This suggests that the economy absorbs immigrants by expanding job opportunities rather than by displacing workers born in the United States."[90] "The U.S. economy is dynamic," Peri concludes, shedding and creating hundreds of thousands of jobs every month. Businesses are in a continuous state of flux. The most accurate way to gauge the net impact of immigration on such an economy is to analyze the effects dynamically over time. Data show that, on net, immigrants expand the U.S. economy's productive capacity, stimulate investment, and promote specialization that in the long run boosts productivity. Consistent with previous research, there is no evidence that these effects take place at the expense of jobs for workers born in the United States.[91]

Conclusion

In this chapter I have cited empirical studies to refute the claims that undocumented immigrants are causing a population explosion, setting off a crime wave, and negatively affecting the economy. As we have seen, the data have demonstrated the following conclusions: (1) the population increase is relatively small in terms of the overall native population, and the current rate of increase is among the lowest in U.S. history; (2) there is simply no basis to conclude that immigrants are more likely to foster a terrorist or criminal element than the native population; and (3) undocumented immigrants have a marked positive fiscal impact and do not lower wages or take away domestic jobs.

On a broader scale, both sides of the immigration debate tend to avoid the difficult questions. For instance, anti-immigrant advocates largely fail to acknowledge the positive economic impact undocumented workers have on the national economies; by the same token, pro-immigrant advocates tend to avoid struggling with the economic strain undocumented workers can place on local and state economies, particularly with respect to elementary and secondary school education as well as increased healthcare costs resulting from fairly rapid growths in populations.[92] While it may be the case that in the long run, the benefits of undocumented workers outweigh any short-term costs deriving from their migration, such an answer often provides little solace for local officials confronting calls by their constituents for immediate efforts to curb immigration. Instead of proposing reasoned reform or federal governmental assistance, state and local responses tend to be efforts to implement restrictive enforcement, which more often than not are precluded by federal preemption doctrines.[93]

A goal of this book is to change the tenor of the current anti-immigration debate, which all too often is clouded by racist and venomous attacks. Unless the attacks cease to victimize Latinos and Latinas in general, and undocumented workers in particular, polarization will just continue, and it will be extraordinarily difficult for any politician or public policy advocate to engage in reasoned and honest debate concerning the economy and the law.[94] The likely result will be that the struggles will continue until one side merely outnumbers the other. In other words, a primary goal of this book is to create space for legitimate debate, based upon facts and data, in an effort to address one of the most significant public policy issues of our day.

4

Immigration's Effects on State and Local Economies

Though scholars have refuted claims that immigration is detrimental to the national economy, arguments about immigration's negative effects on local and state economies carry considerably greater force.[1] Simple logic suggests that healthcare and K-12 education for undocumented immigrants and their families impose increased costs on state and local economies, at least in the short term.

K-12 education costs have always been paid, for the most part, by state and local governments. Moreover, in the famous *Plyler v. Doe* decision in 1982, the U.S. Supreme Court ruled that "children may not be denied education on the basis of their immigration status."[2] The healthcare burdens on states and localities have increased significantly since 1996, when Congress passed two pieces of legislation that drastically limited access to public assistance, including healthcare, for undocumented immigrants: the Illegal Immigration Reform and Immigrant Responsibility Act and the Personal Responsibility and Work Opportunity Reconciliation Act. These laws had many far-reaching consequences. For example, undocumented immigrants were now ineligible for many federal public assistance programs, including Medicaid.[3] States no longer received federal healthcare funding for undocumented immigrants; and even immigrants with legal status were ineligible for Medicaid if they had resided in the country for fewer than five years.[4] Moreover, states now had to require medical professionals to report a patient's immigration status.[5] These measures, while intended to curb immigration, merely shifted the burden to the local and state economies where undocumented immigrants resided (see table 4.1 for the state-by-state distribution of the undocumented immigrant population).

Modifying these legislative measures is a key component of my proposal to ease the effects of undocumented immigration on states and local economies. As we saw in the previous chapter, multiple studies have concluded that immigrants confer a net benefit on the economy of the nation as a whole:

> At the federal level, . . . revenues from immigrants equal or exceed spending on immigrants. Moreover, on a longer-term basis, the lifetime earnings of immigrants, most of whom arrive in America at post school-age and without elderly parents eligible for Social Security and Medicare, are likely to exceed the lifetime government spending they claim.[6]

The federal government needs to transfer these net benefits to state and local governments to reimburse them for the added expenses associated with increased undocumented immigration. I will discuss this proposal in more detail in the book's concluding chapter.

Studies on the Local Impact of Immigration

The influential 1997–1998 National Research Council report, discussed extensively in chapter 3, also weighed in on the issue of immigration's local impacts. As described in a later report by the New Policy Institute,

> [The] study by the National Research Council . . . measured the fiscal impact of immigrants on states and localities, based on estimated costs in New Jersey and California; and . . . found that immigrants generate

TABLE 4.1

State of Residence of the Unauthorized Immigrant Population:
January 2006 and 2000

	Estimated population in January		Percent of total		Percent change	Average annual change
	2000	2006	2000	2006	2000 to 2006	2000 to 2006
All states	11,550,000	8,460,000	100	100	37	515,000
California	2,830,000	2,510,000	25	30	13	53,333
Texas	1,640,000	1,090,000	14	13	50	91,667
Florida	980,000	800,000	8	9	23	30,000
Illinois	550,000	440,000	5	5	25	18,333
New York	540,000	540,000	5	6	-	-
Arizona	500,000	330,000	4	4	52	28,333
Georgia	490,000	220,000	4	3	123	45,000
New Jersey	430,000	350,000	4	4	23	13,333
North Carolina	370,000	260,000	3	3	42	18,333
Washington	280,000	170,000	2	2	65	18,333
Other states	2,950,000	1,750,000	26	21	69	200,000

Source: Michael Hoefer, Nancy Rytina, and Christopher Campbell, "Estimates of the Unau-
thorized Immigrant Population Residing in the United States: January 2006," Department of
Homeland Security, Office of Immigration Statistics, August 2007, http://www.dhs.gov/xli-
brary/assets/statistics/publications/ill_pe_2006.pdf.

a net state and local fiscal burden equivalent to between $166 and $226 per-native household, or less than one-half of one percent of average household income. Furthermore, the analysis found that immigration also produced a net fiscal contribution or surplus at the federal level, . . . [and] that the average immigrant household in New Jersey and California made an estimated net, annual contribution to the federal budget of $520 and $127, respectively.[7]

In 2004 the General Accounting Office issued two reports that attempted to analyze undocumented immigrants' impact on school and hospital costs. In both cases, the authors were hamstrung by a lack of data. The major finding of the GAO report "Illegal Alien Schoolchildren: Issues in Estimating State-by-State Costs" was simply that reliable data are unavailable:

> the government information that is available is not sufficient to reliably quantify the costs of educating illegal alien schoolchildren. All approaches to estimating these costs require data or estimates of the number of illegal alien schoolchildren. Neither state nor local governments collect this information, and federal agencies do not provide estimates.[8]

Similarly, because hospitals "generally do not collect information on patients' immigration status," lack of reliable data was also a major issue in the GAO report "Undocumented Aliens: Questions Persist about Their Impact on Hospitals' Uncompensated Care Costs":

> Despite hospitals' long-standing concern about the costs of treating undocumented aliens, the extent to which these patients affect hospitals' uncompensated care costs remains unknown. The lack of reliable data on this patient population and lack of proven methods to estimate their numbers make it difficult to determine the extent to which hospitals treat undocumented aliens and the costs of their care.[9]

Despite the challenges involved in calculating the cost of undocumented immigrants to local and state economies in terms of education and healthcare, a number of research organizations have conducted studies on individual states, often using population estimates tabulated by the former Immigration and Naturalization Service and the Pew Hispanic Center. For instance, in 2000 the organization Hispanic Advocacy and Community Empowerment through Research released a study on the economic impact of undocumented workers in Minnesota, which reached several largely pro-immigrant conclusions:

> Undocumented immigrants in Minnesota play a critical role in maintaining economic growth and employment opportunities for native

Minnesotans. If the undocumented workers were suddenly removed, Minnesota would experience a 40% decline in economic growth. Even if one believes that the indirect effects of input-output analysis overestimate the value of undocumented workers, the direct effects alone still sum to almost $1.3 billion.[10]

A 2006 report by the New Mexico Fiscal Policy Project used two different estimates for the undocumented immigrant population of New Mexico, one from the INS and one from the Pew Hispanic Center; either estimate yielded the conclusion that undocumented immigrants paid more in sales, property, and income tax than the state paid to educate their children.[11] Similarly, a 2006 study from the Oregon Center for Public Policy pointed out the "significant contributions" made by undocumented workers:

> The labor of undocumented workers is crucial to certain industries. They purchase products and services in Oregon with the roughly $2 billion in income they earn annually. Finally, they are taxpayers, contributing millions of dollars annually to Oregon's tax base and to the federal Social Security and Medicare systems. These taxes paid by undocumented workers total about $137 million to $160 million annually. Taxes paid by Oregon employers on behalf of undocumented workers total about $100 million to $117 million annually.[12]

A 2007 study by the Iowa Policy Project also concluded that undocumented immigrants are not detrimental to the state economy:

> It is important to recognize the fiscal contributions of undocumented immigrants living in Iowa. Undocumented immigrants pay an estimated aggregate amount of $40 million to $62 million in state taxes each year. As a group, undocumented immigrant families earning $27,400 a year pay less in state taxes than do their documented peers in Iowa; however, even an undocumented family sending home remittances and avoiding state income taxes will pay more than $1,300 into the state coffers each year.

Although their tax payments are approximately 80 percent of the taxes paid by legally documented families with comparable incomes, undocumented immigrant families are eligible for far fewer state and federal services than are documented residents in Iowa. In fact, some of their tax payments go to providing state services that undocumented immigrants themselves cannot access because of their immigration status. Employers in Iowa contribute an additional $1.8 million to $2.8 million in state unemployment insurance premiums on behalf of their undocumented employees, who can never access these benefits. Undocumented immigrants working on the books in Iowa and their employers also contribute annually an estimated $50 million to $77.8 million in federal Social Security and Medicare taxes from which they will never benefit. Rather than draining state resources, undocumented immigrants are in some cases subsidizing services that only documented residents can access.[13]

Other studies, particularly those focusing on California, have reached very different conclusions, finding that undocumented immigrants are a drain to state and local economies. This has long been the claim advanced by the Federation for American Immigration Reform (FAIR). In reports like "The Costs of Illegal Immigration to Californians" (2004) and "Breaking the Piggy Bank" (2005), FAIR's authors rely on questionable assumptions, for example, that undocumented workers lower wages and displace native-born workers.[14] Moreover, given the group's connections with extremist anti-immigrant and racist individuals and groups (as discussed in chapter 2), it is difficult to give much credence to FAIR publications. However, reputable economists like Philip J. Romero also conclude that undocumented immigrants are a drain on the California economy. "The average illegal immigrant [in California] receives eight to twelve dollars in services for every dollar they pay in taxes," Romero argued in a 2007 article for the *Social Contract*. "Illegal immigrants impose a multi-billion dollar burden on California taxpayers."[15]

The effect of undocumented immigration on the economies of state and local governments remains a contested issue, particularly because only a limited number of studies have examined the topic. However, those who are concerned about the increase in costs to economies due to undocumented immigration have credible arguments. If these arguments were to be used properly, rather than being used to demonize immigrants, they could help move the federal government to reimburse states for the increased fiscal burdens associated with increased undocumented immigration.

States' Efforts to Implement Immigration Policy

Perhaps in response to frustrations over the costs of undocumented immigration on local economies and federal government inaction, more and more state and local governments have undertaken to address the immigration problem themselves. The Americas Society reports that "between 2005 and 2010, more than 6,000 immigration-related bills were introduced in the 50 state legislatures and more than 1,000 of those bills were enacted."[16] For instance, in 2006 the city of Farmers Branch, Texas, explored various measures to curb immigration in the city, "including prohibiting landlords from leasing to illegal immigrants, penalizing businesses that employ them, making English the city's official language and ceasing publication of any documents in Spanish, and eliminating subsidies for illegal immigrants in the city's youth programs."[17] Such efforts, however, besides being piecemeal and economically unsound, often face legal challenges. An article in the *Brooklyn Law Journal* describes one such example:

In 2005, in the towns of New Ipswich and Hudson, New Hampshire, local police arrested eight suspected undocumented immigrants on charges of criminal trespass when they failed to provide proper identification. Local police resorted to this tactic after the federal authorities declined to take action against the suspects. On August 12, 2005, however, a state judge dismissed these charges, stating that they represented an unconstitutional attempt to regulate the enforcement of immigration violations. The judge reasoned that the police action violated the supremacy clause because the federal regulation was "so pervasive" that it left no room for supplementation by the states.[18]

In 2011 the Americas Society published the report "The Economic Impact of Immigrant-Related Local Ordinances," one of the first comprehensive studies on the topic. The study examined the fifty-three cities that had passed either restrictive or nonrestrictive immigration-related ordinances between 2006 and 2008 (see table 4.2); the authors defined "restrictive" and "nonrestrictive" as follows:

> restrictive policies . . . at the city level, generally include four types of ordinances: business verification of the immigration status of employees; requirements that landlords verify the immigration status of tenants; 287(g) agreements that give local officials immigration enforcement powers; and English-only. At the state level, restrictive policies extend to cover health care, education, transportation, and other areas under shared state jurisdiction. Still, although fewer in number, other cities and states have opted for non-restrictive policies toward the undocumented immigrant population. These localities, referred to as sanctuary cities, provide access to public services and bar local law enforcement and city employees from investigating the legal status of residents.[19]

The study found that the employment-related restrictive ordinances had a measurable effect on numbers of employees:

> On average, the expected number of employees in a city with a restrictive employment-related ordinance would be approximately 0.26 times lower than the number in a city that enacted a non-restrictive ordinance. For instance, if the number of employees in a city that enacted a non-restrictive ordinance was 10,000, the model predicts, on average, an observation of 2,600 fewer jobs in a city that enacted an employment-restrictive ordinance.[20]

A few other studies have analyzed the impact of local legislation on specific states; these will be discussed in the following sections.

TABLE 4.2

Immigrant-Related Ordinances, by City and Type (2006–2008)

CITY	STATE	ORDINANCE	YEAR PASSED	TYPE
Oakland	CA	Non-Restrictive	2007	Sanctuary
Santa Cruz	CA	Non-Restrictive	2007	Sanctuary
Watsonville	CA	Non-Restrictive	2007	Sanctuary
Hartford	CT	Non-Restrictive	2008	Sanctuary
New Haven	CT	Non-Restrictive	2007	Sanctuary
Chicago	IL	Non-Restrictive	2006	Sanctuary
Chelsea	MA	Non-Restrictive	2007	Sanctuary
Detroit	MI	Non-Restrictive	2007	Sanctuary
Carrboro	NC	Non-Restrictive	2006	Sanctuary
Chapel Hill	NC	Non-Restrictive	2007	Sanctuary
Newark	NJ	Non-Restrictive	2006	Sanctuary
Alexandria	VA	Non-Restrictive	2006	Sanctuary
Middlebury	VT	Non-Restrictive	2007	Sanctuary
Athens	AL	Restrictive	2007	Employment
Gadsden	AL	Restrictive	2006	English-only
Rogers	AR	Restrictive	2007	287(g)
Springdale	AR	Restrictive	2007	287(g)
Lake Havasu City	AZ	Restrictive	2007	Employment
Payson	AZ	Restrictive	2007	Employment
Phoenix	AZ	Restrictive	2008	287(g)
Apple Valley	CA	Restrictive	2006	Employment
Lancaster	CA	Restrictive	2007	Employment
Mission Viejo	CA	Restrictive	2007	Employment
Santa Clarita	CA	Restrictive	2006	Employment
Vista	CA	Restrictive	2007	Employment
Cape Coral	FL	Restrictive	2006	Employment
Barnstable Town	MA	Restrictive	2006	Housing
Taneytown	MD	Restrictive	2006	English-only
Hazel Park	MI	Restrictive	2006	English-only
Valley Park	MO	Restrictive	2007	Employment

TABLE 4.2 *(continued)*

CITY	STATE	ORDINANCE	YEAR PASSED	TYPE
Durham	NC	Restrictive	2008	287(g)
Landis	NC	Restrictive	2006	English-only
Sou×thern Shores	NC	Restrictive	2008	English-only
Las Vegas	NV	Restrictive	2008	287(g)
Bellaire	OH	Restrictive	2007	Employment
Sycamore Township	OH	Restrictive	2007	Employment
Inola	OK	Restrictive	2006	Employment
Oologah	OK	Restrictive	2006	Employment
Tulsa	OK	Restrictive	2006	Employment
Altoona	PA	Restrictive	2006	Employment
Berwick	PA	Restrictive	2007	Housing
Bridgeport	PA	Restrictive	2006	Housing
Gilberton	PA	Restrictive	2006	Employment
Mahanoy City	PA	Restrictive	2006	Employment
Shenandoah	PA	Restrictive	2006	English-only
Beaufort	SC	Restrictive	2006	Employment
Gaston	SC	Restrictive	2006	Employment
Carrollton	TX	Restrictive	2008	287(g)
Farmers Branch	TX	Restrictive	2008	287(g)
Herndon	VA	Restrictive	2007	287(g)
Manassas	VA	Restrictive	2008	287(g)
Manassas Park	VA	Restrictive	2008	287(g)
Green Bay	WI	Restrictive	2007	Employment

Source: Americas Society, "The Economic Impact of Immigrant-Related Local Ordinances," 2011, 13, http://www.as-coa.org/sites/default/files/ASImmigrationWhitePaper.pdf. Reprinted by permission.

State-Level Efforts to Implement Restrictive Immigration Policies

Bills like Arizona's SB 1070, Georgia's HB 87, and Alabama's HB 56 are aimed at limiting undocumented immigrants' access to jobs and public services, but in some cases they have undoubtedly fueled discrimination toward immigrants and Latinas and Latinos overall. It will be useful to revisit these findings in coming years, as the long-term impacts of immigration-related ordinances become more apparent. The fact that the effect of restrictive ordinances may be felt more in industries that traditionally employ larger numbers of immigrants does not necessarily imply that other members of society will not feel any deleterious effects.

Arizona made headlines in April 2010 when Governor Jan Brewer signed into law the Support Our Law Enforcement and Safe Neighborhoods Act, known as Arizona Senate Bill 1070. A helpful summary of the law and the legal challenges it faced can be found at the U.S. Supreme Court's blog:

> The Arizona legislature passed S.B. 1070 . . . because it believes that the federal government has not done enough to combat illegal immigration. The official goal of the law is "attrition by enforcement"—that is, putting strict controls on illegal immigrants in the hope that they will become fed up and return to their home countries. Before the law went into effect in 2010, the federal government went to court to block the state from enforcing the law, arguing that federal immigration law trumped, or "preempted," the state law. The lower courts agreed with the federal government, and late last year [2011] the Supreme Court granted the state's request for review.
>
> Four different provisions of S.B. 1070 are currently [April 2012] before the Court. One provision, Section 2(B), requires police officers to check the immigration status of anyone whom they arrest; it also allows police to stop and arrest anyone whom they believe to be an illegal immigrant. Section 3 makes it a crime for someone even to be in the state without valid immigration papers, while Section 5(C) makes it a crime to apply for or hold a job in Arizona without proper papers. Finally, in Section 6, the law

gives a police officer the power to arrest someone, without a warrant, if the officer believes that he has committed a crime that could cause him to be deported, no matter where the crime may have occurred.[21]

Many other objections to SB 1070 have been raised; the Immigration Policy Center provides a representative sample:

> This bill, if it becomes law, will likely affect not only unauthorized immigrants, but all immigrants and Latinos in general. Given the vital role that immigrants and Latinos play in Arizona's economy, and considering Arizona's current budget deficit of $3 billion, enacting SB 1070 could be a perilous move.
>
> At a purely administrative level, Gov. Brewer should take into consideration the potential costs of implementation and defending the state against lawsuits. As the National Employment Law Project (NELP) points out in the case of other states that have passed harsh local immigration laws, Arizona would probably face a costly slew of lawsuits on behalf of legal immigrants and native-born Latinos who feel they have been unjustly targeted. This is in addition to the cost of implementation. . . .
>
> More broadly, Gov. Brewer should keep in mind that, if significant numbers of immigrants and Latinos are actually persuaded to leave the state because of this new law, they will take their tax dollars, businesses, and purchasing power with them. The University of Arizona's Udall Center for Studies in Public Policy estimates that the total economic output attributable to Arizona's immigrant workers was $44 billion in 2004, which sustained roughly 400,000 full-time jobs. Furthermore, over 35,000 businesses in Arizona are Latino-owned and had sales and receipts of $4.3 billion and employed 39,363 people in 2002, the last year for which data is available. The Perryman Group estimates that if all unauthorized immigrants were removed from Arizona, the state would lose $26.4 billion in economic activity, $11.7 billion in gross state product, and approximately 140,324 jobs, even accounting for adequate market adjustment time. Putting economic contributions

of this magnitude at risk during a time of recession would not serve Arizona well.[22]

A 2010 study by the National Immigration Forum also listed various issues raised by the bill:

> Several key policy and public safety questions surrounding Arizona's new law remain unanswered by proponents. For example, independent analyses of the potential cost of the new law to the state have demonstrated that it is prohibitively expensive. Add in Arizona's already massive budget deficit, and it's hard to see how Arizona can afford to enforce its new law. Additionally, the new law triggered a national backlash that hurt the state's tourism and convention industry, exacerbating Arizona's already severe budget and economic woes. Multiple lawsuits triggered by the legislation will cost the state millions as it will have to defend the new law in court.[23]

In 2011 the Center for American Progress and the Immigration Policy Center released a major report on the economic impact of Arizona's SB 1070. The report addressed two fundamental questions:

> If S.B. 1070–type laws accomplish the declared goal of driving out all undocumented immigrants, what effect would it actually have on state economies? And conversely, what would the impact be on state economies if undocumented immigrants acquired legal status?
>
> The economic analysis in this report shows the S.B. 1070 approach would have devastating economic consequences if its goals were accomplished. When undocumented workers are taken out of the economy, the jobs they support through their labor, consumption, and tax payments disappear as well. . . .
>
> In contrast, were undocumented immigrants to acquire legal status, their wages and productivity would increase, they would spend more in our economy and pay more in taxes, and new jobs would be created.[24]

The report lists the following consequences of mass deportation from Arizona:

- Decrease total employment by 17.2 percent
- Eliminate 581,000 jobs for immigrant and native-born workers alike
- Shrink state economy by $48.8 billion
- Reduce state tax revenues by 10.1 percent[25]

In contrast, these are the projected results if undocumented immigrants in Arizona were granted legal status:

- Increase total employment by 7.7 percent
- Add 261,000 jobs for immigrant and native-born workers alike
- Increase labor income by $5.6 billion
- Increase tax revenues by $1.68 billion[26]

In June 2012 the Supreme Court handed down its decision in *Arizona v. United States*:

> the Court held that three of the four provisions of the law at issue in the case cannot go into effect at all because they are "preempted," or trumped, by federal immigration laws. And while the Court allowed one provision—which requires police officers to check the immigration status of anyone whom they detain or arrest before they release that person—to go into effect, even here it left open the possibility that this provision would eventually be held unconstitutional if not applied narrowly in Arizona.[27]

Despite the legal challenges facing Arizona's bill, both Georgia and Alabama passed similar legislation during the first half of 2011. Georgia's HB 87, enacted in April 2011, is essentially the East Coast equivalent of Arizona's cowboy-style SB 1070.[28] According to the *Atlanta Journal Constitution*,

Republican Rep. Matt Ramsey's bill would punish people who encourage illegal immigrants to enter the state and punish people who transport and conceal them when they get here. Supporters say the state needs to take action because illegal immigrants are sapping taxpayer-funded resources and taking jobs amid high unemployment. . . . Critics say the legislation could hurt Georgia's economy, particularly its $65 billion agricultural industry, which relies heavily on migrant workers.[29]

Alabama's HB 56, enacted in June 2011, "empowers law enforcement officials to check the immigration status of individuals, makes it a crime to knowingly transport an undocumented immigrant and requires school officials to determine the immigration status of students and their parents, among other provisions."[30] The Southern Poverty Law Center has called it "the harshest such law to be enacted by any state."[31] Samuel Addy, a professor of economics at the University of Alabama, estimated that, as a result of HB 56, between forty thousand and eighty thousand undocumented workers would leave the state:

> The resulting decline in aggregate demand would have annual economic and fiscal impacts of reductions of about (i) 70,000–140,000 jobs with $1.2–5.8 billion in earnings, (ii) $2.3–10.8 billion in Alabama GDP or 1.3–6.2 percent of the state's $172.6 billion GDP in 2010, (iii) $56.7–264.5 million in state income and sales tax collections, and (iv) $20.0–93.1 million in local sales tax collections.[32]

"Instead of boosting state economic growth," Addy concluded, "the law is certain to be a drag on economic development."[33]

Indeed, there are several efforts afoot seeking the law's repeal, including local business executives as well as Democratic state senator Billy Beasley, who said that the law "has created a world of hurt for our state. . . . HB 56 is just a mean-spirited law—period."[34]

Business and economic development leaders in Alabama have joined calls for reform of the state's immigration law after a Tuscaloosa police officer arrested a Mercedes-Benz manager because he did not have his driver's license with him. The arrest of a German executive from the company that launched Alabama's thriving auto industry and is poised to expand its sizeable operations in Tuscaloosa County has prompted some lawmakers to acknowledge that the law has had "unintended consequences" and needs reform.

Business leaders like David Bronner, chief executive of the Retirement Systems of Alabama, are concerned that the immigration law is revealing Alabama to be an unwelcoming place for foreign investors. . . .

Mr. Bronner said that the law gives the impression that Alabama officials "don't like foreigners, period."[35]

One of the more controversial provisions of Alabama's law is Section 28, which requires public schools to record the immigration status of incoming students and their parents. What is perhaps most disturbing about the section is that it is intended to serve as the basis for an eventual challenge to the Supreme Court ruling in *Plyler v. Doe*, as reported by the *New York Times*:

Michael M. Hethmon, general counsel for the Immigration Reform Law Institute in Washington, who wrote the provision, insists that its goal is much more ambitious.

The eventual target, he said, is the 1982 Supreme Court decision *Plyler v. Doe*. The case concerned a Texas statute that withheld funds for the education of illegal immigrants and allowed districts to bar them from enrollment, as well as one Texas school district's plan to charge illegal immigrants tuition.

The court ruled that this violated the Constitution's equal protection clause, saying that the statute "imposes a lifetime hardship on a discrete class of children not accountable" for their immigration status. In the decision, the court also said that the state had not presented evidence showing it was substantially harmed by giving these children—as distinct from any other children—a free public education.

Over the ensuing decades, measures have been passed in defiance of this ruling, most notably California's Proposition 187, but they have been repeatedly struck down in the courts. Mr. Hethmon said the problem with these challenges is that they have not taken the trouble to gather the evidence the court found missing in *Plyler*.

"The toughest question has been obtaining reliable—and I mean reliable for peer-reviewed research purposes—censuses of the number of illegal alien students enrolled in school districts," he said. "That information could be compared with other sorts of performance or resource allocation issues."

The Alabama law directs schools to ascertain the immigration status of incoming students, through a birth certificate, other official documents or an affidavit by the child's parents (the law also directs schools to determine the immigration status of an enrolling child's parents, but gave no mechanism by which to do so).

That information is then passed on to the State Board of Education not only to prepare an annual report with the data but also to "contract with reputable scholars and research institutions" to determine the costs, fiscal and otherwise, of educating illegal immigrants.

Because no one is actually barred from attending school and the data is not passed on to law enforcement, the provision passes constitutional muster, Mr. Hethmon said.

But it also potentially enables a fresh challenge to *Plyler v. Doe*, and the idea that schools are obligated to provide a free education to illegal immigrants.[36]

Various provisions of Georgia's HB 87 and Alabama's HB 56, including Section 28, were blocked by a federal appeals court in August 2012:

The court rejected Georgia's effort to criminalize transporting and harboring illegal immigrants and to make it illegal to "induce or entice" them to enter the state—a crime that has no parallel in federal law. It also blocked Section 28 of Alabama's law, which requires schools to collect information about students' immigration status. The court sensibly said this would deter children from entering school, violating the Supreme Court's 1982 ruling in *Plyler v. Doe* that guarantees all children the right to an elementary education.

The court, however, upheld the sections of laws in both states that allow police officers to check the immigration papers of people they stop—provisions that invite racial profiling. But as the Supreme Court did in its Arizona ruling, it left open the possibility of future challenges on civil-rights or due-process grounds.[37]

Despite legal setbacks, it seems clear that states and localities will continue to pass immigration-related laws until Congress resolves the matter once and for all. The citizens of Arizona, Georgia, and Alabama are experiencing the detrimental effects of the anti-immigrant measures firsthand. Most notable is the reduction in available workers, causing labor shortages, which in turn result in rotting crops, delayed construction projects, and higher prices for these services that are becoming scarcer as a result of the legislation.

DREAM Act Legislation at the Federal and State Levels

The term DREAM Act refers to the proposed federal legislation that has languished in Congress for over a decade—the Development, Relief, and Education for Alien Minors (DREAM) Act. Some state legislatures have passed similar legislation, as summarized by Carl Krueger, a policy analyst at the Education Commission of the States:

> In an effort to aid undocumented immigrants who cannot afford the cost of postsecondary education, many states have proposed legislation that offers in-state tuition to this new pool of potential students. Supporters of this legislation point out that most of the children of undocumented immigrants are in the United States to stay, and by providing them access to postsecondary education, society benefits as a whole through increased earnings and taxes, and lower crime and poverty rates.

Supporters also draw on the long history of immigration to the United States and argue it is unfair to deny opportunity to the most recent generation of undocumented aliens. Critics argue it is unfair to allocate in-state tuition to illegal aliens at a time when many American citizens cannot afford to attend postsecondary education. While some states have passed legislation that extends in-state tuition to undocumented immigrants, others have proposed laws that restrict the awarding of in-state tuition to these same immigrants.[38]

Republican U.S. Senator Orrin Hatch, an author of earlier versions of the federal DREAM Act, made a compelling argument for it in 2003:

Many of these youngsters find themselves caught in a catch-22 situation, as [undocumented] immigrants, they cannot work legally and they are also effectively barred from developing academically beyond high school because of the high cost of pursuing higher education. In short, although these children have built their lives here, they have no possibility of achieving and living the American dream. What a tremendous loss. . . . What a tremendous loss to our society.[39]

In his recent book *No Undocumented Child Left Behind*, Michael Olivas provides a detailed history of the many failed attempts to pass the federal DREAM Act:

Following the introduction of the DREAM Act in 2001, in both 2003 and 2005, the DREAM Act was reintroduced in Congress, and in 2004, Senate Judicial Committee hearings were held. The bill languished there until comprehensive immigration-reform efforts failed in summer 2007. . . . In one last attempt in the session to enact legislation to address the status of the college students, on October 24, 2007, the Senate considered and voted down the stand-alone DREAM Act, 44–52, on the cloture motion; three years later, a similar cloture vote was defeated, when on September 21, 2010, the DREAM Act (S. 3454, the National

Defense Authorization Act for Fiscal Year 2011) was defeated 43–56. . . . Senator Reid . . . [again introduced] the legislation during the lame-duck session in December 2010, after Democrats lost control of the House and kept a thin majority in the Senate. Not even one Republican senator voted for the legislation, not even those who had supported and introduced it earlier.[40]

Texas has had its own version of the DREAM Act since 2001, when HB 1403 was enacted. The commentator Mark Whittington provided a useful overview of the legislation on its tenth anniversary in 2011:

- The bill amended the Texas education code to classify an alien living in the U.S. who has petitioned the INS for legal status to be treated the same as an American citizen for the purpose of those who qualify for resident status for tuition and fee purposes. . . .
- The bill exempted foreign students from paying foreign student tuition if they were citizens of a nation adjacent to Texas (i.e. Mexico), registered in an academic teaching institution or junior college, and met the qualifications of Texas residency provided by the bill.
- The main argument for the bill was that it would provide a more equitable access to institutions of higher education to children of illegal aliens who were attempting to legalize their status. Thus the pool of skilled, educated workers would increase, saving Texas money in the long run. Discriminating against children of illegal immigrants who entered the country through no fault of their own was said to be unfair.
- The main argument against the bill was that it would turn a blind eye to law breaking (i.e. residing in the country illegally), would be unfair to students who reside in Texas legally, and would cost the state a considerable amount of money. Finally, the law is said to provide a magnet for illegal aliens to enter the United States to provide an education for their children.[41]

Summing up, Whittington noted, "All attempts to repeal or amend the Texas Dream Act in the Texas Legislature have so far failed."

In 2011 California passed its version of the DREAM Act as well:

The California Dream Act consists of two bills. . . . AB 131 allows undocumented college students who meet state residency requirements to apply for Cal Grants and other publicly-funded tuition assistance, the same available to other students; AB 130 . . . allows them to apply for private grants and scholarships they could not access before. Until now, California college students who are in the U.S. illegally, many brought here as minors, have been barred from public financial aid.[42]

As reported by *PBS NewsHour,*

There has been an outpouring of response to the latest bill from both supporters and opponents. The legislation has been highly controversial in a state with a severe economic and budget crisis. . . . Gov. Brown and supporters of the Dream Act claim that young people who qualify should have the opportunity to get a college education and do more than "just sweeping floors." Some opponents, however, say that even with a college education, undocumented graduates won't be able to start careers anyway because of their status.[43]

In 2006 Carl Krueger surveyed the various state-level legislative proposals related to higher education for undocumented immigrants: "Thirty states have considered legislation that would allow undocumented immigrants to receive in-state tuition," he reported. Of those,

nine states have passed laws that allow undocumented immigrants to receive in-state tuition: California, Illinois, Kansas, New Mexico, New York, Oklahoma, Texas, Utah and Washington. . . . Six states—Alaska, Arizona, Colorado, North Carolina, Utah and Virginia—have tried to pass legislation that would ban undocumented immigrants from receiving in-state tuition. So far, none of these efforts have been successful.[44]

Krueger summarized his findings in a list of state legislative bills, depicting whether they awarded or restricted benefits to undocumented students, and whether or not they were passed (see table 4.3). Though the data were collected in 2006, the table is a useful indication that states are becoming aware of the need to act on education-related immigrant assistance programs.

The Tragedy of the Commons

The effects of undocumented immigration on state and local governments are still a matter of debate, fueled in part by a lack of reliable data and an abundance of heated rhetoric. While the few studies on the matter are in conflict, it appears that undocumented immigrants, at least in the short term, impose costs to the state related to healthcare and K-12 education. On the other hand, attempts to pass state-level immigration policies have met with legal challenges and opposition by business leaders as well as human rights activists.

If logic prevails, all sides of the debate will recognize the overall positive impact of undocumented immigrants. Moreover, through certain taxes, undocumented immigrants may be able to reimburse those states with large undocumented populations, especially if those states can obtain reimbursement from the federal government for additional healthcare and education costs.

The other parties that may help address the strain on state and local governments are the free riders in the national immigration debate— domestic business sectors that create the demand for undocumented immigrants. Industries like agriculture, service, construction, and food processing have long benefited from undocumented immigration. Domestic businesses that create this free rider situation must take their appropriate responsibility and play a legitimate role in addressing the immigration debate in this country.

In a 2008 *Indiana Law Journal* article coauthored with Christopher B. Carbot, I discussed the rationale for and consequences of free riding:

> The concept of freeriding, also referred to as the tragedy of the commons, is a theory of communal resource use often applied in property law and microeconomics. One common example of this concept, which

TABLE 4.3
State Legislative Bills Related to Education for
Undocumented Students (2006)

State	Policy	Award	Restrict	Passed?
Alaska	H.B. 39 (2003)		X	No
Arizona	H.B. 2518 (2003)	X		No
	H.B 2392 (2004)		X	No
	H.B. 2069 (2006)		X	Proposed
Arkansas	H.B. 1525 (2005)	X		No
California	A.B. 540 (2001)	X		Yes
Colorado	H.B. 1178 (2003)	X		No
	H.B. 1187 (2004)		X	No
Connecticut	H.B. 6793 (2005)	X		Proposed
Delaware	H.B. 222 (2003)	X		No
	H.R. 59 (2004)	X[208]		Yes
Florida	H.B. 27 (2003)	X		No
	H.B. 119 (2003)	X		No
Georgia	H.B. 1810 (2001)	X		No
Hawaii	H.B. 873 (2003)	X		No
Illinois	H.B. 60 (2003)	X		Yes
Kansas	H.B. 2145 (2004)	X		Yes
Maryland	H.B. 253 (2003)	X		Vetoed
Massachusetts	S.B. 237 (2003)	X		Vetoed
	H.B. 3924 (2004)	X		No
Minnesota	S.B. 3027 (2002)	X		No
Mississippi	H.B. 101 (2005)	X		No
	H.B. 88 (2006)	X		No
Missouri	S.B. 296 (2005)	X		Proposed
Nebraska	L.B. 152 (2003)	X		No
New Jersey	S.B. 78 (2004)	X		No
	S.B. 436 (2006)			Proposed
New Mexico	S.B. 582 (2005)	X		Yes
New York	S.B. 7784 (2002)	X		Yes
North Carolina	S.B. 982 (2003)		X	No

TABLE 4.3 (continued)

State	Policy	Award	Restrict	Passed?
	H.B. 1183 (2005)	X		Proposed
Oklahoma	S.B. 596 (2003)	X		Yes
Oregon	S.B. 769 (2005)	X		Proposed
Rhode Island	H.B. 6184 (2005)	X		Proposed
Texas	H.B. 1403 (2001)	X		Yes
Utah	H.B. 331 (2002)	X		Yes
	H.B. 7 (2006)		X	Proposed
Virginia	H.B. 2339 (2003)		X	Vetoed
	H.B. 156 (2004)		X[209]	No
	S.B. 677 (2006)	X		Proposed
	H.B. 262 (2006)		X[210]	No
	H.B. 1050 (2006)		X	No
Washington	H.B. 1079 (2003)	X		Yes
Wisconsin	A.B. 95 (2003)	X		No

Source: Carl Krueger, "In-State Tuition for Undocumented Immigrants," Education Commission of the States, State Notes, August 2006, 2–3, http://www.ecs.org/clearinghouse/61/00/6100. htm#_edn1. Reprinted by permission.

is a twist on the classic tragedy of the commons example, is that of pollution, where individuals decide it is less economically burdensome for them to simply dump waste in the commons than to purify and dispose of it in a more sanitary manner. Essentially, this individual's rationale for his actions are that the cost society at-large will bear because of his actions is much less than the cost he would individually bear to dispose of his waste properly. However, as other individuals follow suit, the aggregate result is that the commons are destroyed. The individuals conveniently dumping their waste may have enjoyed an individual benefit in that their domain is waste-free at a lower cost than otherwise possible, but it has come at the expense of the entire commons becoming a wasteland. In other words, the externalities borne upon the rest of the society ultimately result in a greater long-term loss. The problem associated with such externalities created by individuals or enterprises

and their impact on society at large has also been the subject of litiga-
tion, especially with respect to pollution and other environmental dam-
age caused by industrial operations.[45]

The next logical question is that if in fact certain domestic business
sectors are free riders, why should they change their status? And if they
were interested in doing so, how would they do so? The answer to these
queries is that domestic business sectors should recognize their free
rider status because it would ultimately serve their interests. Instead of
the current costly and dangerous state of affairs, where domestic businesses have to avoid being raided by federal ICE officials, their status
can be embraced at, in all probability, substantial savings. Instead of
fearing work stoppages resulting from ICE raids, these domestic business sectors would be able to operate freely and openly using previously
undocumented workers. There would be substantial savings to domestic
business if such an approach were adopted.

In return for this new freedom, domestic businesses must play—
and more importantly, pay—their part in the immigration equation. In
return for openly hiring and using previously undocumented workers,
these employers would have to incur some of the added costs previously borne by state and local governments. These domestic employers
could reduce the dependency on government healthcare by creating
employee medical centers or subsidizing existing local healthcare facil-
ities. In terms of the added education costs borne by state and local
governments resulting from undocumented immigration, domestic
business could bear some of these costs, but more likely, this is an area
where the federal government could establish a program based on formal requests made by states for their added education expenses. The
above is a preliminary proposal for a reimbursement plan that both
domestic businesses and the federal government can bear, in light of
the benefit from undocumented immigration both sectors currently
enjoy. Details of exactly how such programs would work necessarily
require further analysis.

5

The Conflicted United States–Mexico Relationship

Invitation and Exclusion

Although the United States is often described as a "nation of immigrants,"[1] this country's treatment of Latin American immigrants is
largely a tale of inclusion and assistance on one hand, and exclusion and
mistreatment on the other. As Kevin Johnson succinctly describes it,

> U.S. immigration law is famous for its cyclical, turbulent, and ambiva-
> lent nature. At times, the nation has embraced some of the most liberal
> immigration admission laws and policies in the world. . . . At other times
> in U.S. history, however, the nation has capitulated to the nativist impulse
> and embraced immigration laws and policies that, in retrospect, make us
> cringe with shame and regret.[2]

During earlier periods of exclusion and deportation, popular rhetoric
was filled with characterizations of immigrants that resemble the recent
venomous incarnations.[3] During times of inclusivity, however, the dominant rhetoric of hate did not carry the day.

Interestingly, the U.S. Constitution says virtually nothing concerning
immigration, except for a brief mention of the importation of slaves and

the stipulation that Congress has the power to regulate naturalization.[4] As the legal scholars Paul Brickner and Meghan Hanson note, "for more than one hundred years after our nation's founding, Congress failed to enact legislation that directly addressed immigration."[5] Both the Constitution and the early Congress made laudable proclamations concerning the rights of its inhabitants, but also made clear that African Americans and indigenous peoples were not considered true members of this democracy.[6] Article 1, Section 2, Paragraph 3 of the Constitution provides that "representatives and direct Taxes shall be apportioned among the several States which may be included within this Union, according to their respective Numbers, which shall be determined by adding to the whole Number of free Persons, including those bound to Service for a Term of Years, and excluding Indians not taxed, three fifths of all other Persons."

When Congress eventually acted on immigration, it declared that only "free white persons" were worthy of naturalization, or in other words, citizenship.[7] It was not until 1875 that Congress enacted the first immigration law, forbidding immigration by prostitutes and convicted criminals.[8] In 1882, Congress followed up with laws excluding indigents and other undesirables.[9] As Kevin Johnson observes, "Since comprehensive federal immigration came into place in 1875, the United States has had an unbroken history of immigration laws that restrict immigration and attempt to ensure a certain quality standard among immigrants."[10] With the Immigration Act of 1917, Congress passed legislation containing literacy requirements and assuming the power to deport aliens convicted of specified offenses.[11]

During periods when immigrants were welcomed out of economic necessity, immigrants were viewed as hardworking and reliable; during periods of domestic economic downturns or political tensions such as during or shortly after wars, immigrants were viewed as threats. During the periods of distrust, the negative narratives were typically accompanied by policies targeting immigrants, including mass deportation efforts. Therefore all the hateful rhetoric and scapegoating discussed in the first two chapters are far from new in this country.[12] In times of hostility, immigrants' vulnerability, due to their limited rights, inevitably made them threatened. After all, the threat of deportation always lingers, irrespective of their documented or undocumented status.[13] It is this threat, along with subordinated rights, that makes immigrants among the most vulnerable in our society.

The subsequent pages will address a repeated history of welcoming immigrants when economic conditions necessitated it, but rejecting them when economic conditions or national security matters created an environment of fear and hate. During these cycles, domestic narratives concerning immigrants changed, often quickly. The accounts here serve to demonstrate how past negative narratives often shaped anti-immigrant policies, including attempts at closing the border as well as mass exodus campaigns such as the infamous Operation Wetback of the 1950s. Yet these policies, no matter how draconian, did not put an end to undocumented immigration, particularly when certain sectors of the economy, such as agriculture, were demanding or would eventually once again demand immigrant labor. Moreover, the tried and true approach of demonizing and scapegoating immigrants has not affected demands for immigration labor, and thus has not affected immigration. This country needs to learn from its past, and not merely repeat ineffective measures.

There are many parallels between the experiences of Mexican immigrants and the experiences of immigrants from Asia. Initial policies inviting Mexican laborers were inevitably followed by efforts to oust them, due to a perceived decline in labor demand, or when unrelated events led to isolationist sentiments in the country. During the late nineteenth century and throughout the twentieth century, there were repeated examples of government-sponsored efforts to attract Mexican labor, only to be followed by efforts to deport the very same groups when economic conditions changed, or perceived crises provoked mass hysteria.[14]

Asian immigrants have also repeatedly experienced periods of invitation to meet the country's agricultural demands or build this land's infrastructure and industries. Subsequently this same group confronted domestic efforts to deport them, frequently after not being paid their promised wages.[15] Perhaps the most infamous of these episodes occurred in the late nineteenth century, when federal, state, and local governments used their resources to initially invite but later exclude and deport Chinese immigrants. These efforts led to the passage of the Chinese exclusion laws, which sought to halt all forms of Chinese immigration. In *The Huddled Masses Myth*, Kevin Johnson summarizes the Chinese exclusion laws and their aftermath:

> The Supreme Court emphasized national sovereignty as the rationale for not disturbing the laws that excluded the "obnoxious Chinese" from the United States. In the famous *Chinese Exclusion Case*, the Court stated that "[t]he power of exclusion of foreigners [is] an incident of sovereignty belonging to the government of the United States, as a part of sovereign powers delegated by the Constitution." Similarly, in *Fong Yue Ting v. United States*, the Court reasoned that "[t]he right of a nation to expel or deport foreigners . . . is as absolute and unqualified as the right to prohibit and prevent their entrance into the country."
>
> Congress later extended the Chinese exclusion laws to bar immigration from other Asian nations and to prohibit the immigration of persons of Asian ancestry from any nation. The so-called Gentleman's Agreement between the U.S. and Japanese governments in 1907–1908 greatly restricted immigration from Japan. The Immigration Act of 1917 expanded Chinese exclusion to prohibit immigration from the "Asiatic barred zone." And a 1924 law, best known for creating the discriminatory national origins quota system, allowed for the exclusion of noncitizens "ineligible to citizenship," thus affecting Asian immigrants who, as non-whites, were prohibited from naturalizing.[16]

Immigrants from other regions were affected by these policies as well, as Kevin Johnson notes in *Opening the Floodgates*: "In 1924, Congress imposed strict national-origin quotas on southern and eastern Europeans because of the belief . . . that those immigrants were racially inferior. Through the quota system, Congress sought to restore the racial demographics of the United States as of 1890, a time before the large flow of southern and eastern European immigrants."[17] This national origins system

> restricted annual immigration from any foreign country to 2 percent of that country's population living in the United States, as counted in the census of 1890. Since most of the foreign-born counted in the 1890 census were from northern and western European countries, the 1924 Immigration Act reinforced patterns of white immigration and staved off immigration from other areas, including Asia, Latin America, and Africa.
>
> Until the 1960s, approximately two-thirds of all legal immigrants to the United States were from Europe and Canada.[18]

As Kevin Johnson explains,

> The Supreme Court interpreted the naturalization law, which allowed white immigrants as well as (after the Civil War) persons of African ancestry to naturalize, as barring Asians from naturalizing. In *United States v. Thind*, the Court held that an immigrant from India was not "white" and was therefore ineligible for naturalization. Similarly, in *Ozawa v. United States*, the Court held that, as a nonwhite, a Japanese immigrant could not naturalize.[19]

While the naturalization prerequisite system as well as the immigration quota systems came to an end in the twentieth century, immigration remains a hotly debated issue. The immigration issues of today are all too similar to those of the past, as is this country's conflicted relationship with its southern neighbors.

The United States–Mexico Revolving Door

A glance at the history of U.S.-Mexico relations reveals that from the beginning, the two countries have been involved in territorial disputes, their borders drawn and redrawn as a result of treaties, controversial land purchases, and armed conflict.[20] The history of labor migration between the two countries has been similarly conflicted. After the Mexican-American War, "55,000 migrant workers were brought into the former Mexican territories to work on the railroads between 1850 and 1880."[21] Their expertise as well as their labor power was valued; for example, as I note in my book *Citizenship and Its Exclusions*,

> In the mid-1800s, American society welcomed Mexicans to California in order to learn from them (among other things) Mexican mining techniques. . . . [O]nce the Americans learned those techniques, they began to perceive Mexicans as undesirable foreign competition, and in 1850, the California legislature passed the Foreign Miners Tax to discourage Mexicans from gold mining. As a result of this American perception of Mexican competition and inferiority, coupled with gerrymandering by Americans, Mexican Americans' influence in domestic politics was greatly diminished.[22]

The need for Mexican labor continued in the early twentieth century. As the historian Mae Ngai explains,

> From the turn of the century to World War I, labor flowed more or less freely from Mexico into the United States. Mexican workers provided the human labor power for the region's agricultural revolution and laid the infrastructure for the modern Southwest's economy: they laid railroad tracks that connected the region to the national market, cleared ranch lands for farming, and drug irrigation canals.[23]

With the start of the Mexican Revolution in 1910, as noted by the journalist Tom Head, "over 50,000 Mexican workers immigrated to the United States every year looking for jobs, and our leaders welcomed them with open arms as long as there was a need for them—they proved particularly useful during World War I."[24] This era saw the establishment of the first guest worker program, as described by the legal scholar Alexandra Villarreal O'Rourke:

The concept of a temporary migrant worker program has been in exis-
tence since 1917 when the Department of Labor, responding to a labor crisis brought about by increasingly strict immigration restrictions, created
a guest worker program for agricultural laborers from Mexico. Approximately 72,000 guest workers participated in the program between 1917
and 1921.[25]

Mexico was not subject to the country quotas of the 1924 National
Origins Act that controlled immigration to the United States. As David
Gutiérrez notes, "by the 1920s, Mexican immigrant and Mexican-American workers dominated the unskilled and semi-skilled sectors of the
regional labor market."[26] As I have noted elsewhere, "Mexican American
laborers were not limited to agricultural labor but also participated in
construction, railroad construction and maintenance, and other tasks
that Americans were not willing to perform."[27]

It is important to reiterate that Mexican laborers were welcomed
because they effectively mitigated labor shortages caused by the restrictions on immigrants from Europe and Asia.[28] As Lisa Flores explains,

> Agricultural and industrial businesses working with journalists and polit-
> ical leaders crafted a narrative of need in which Mexicans became posi-
> tioned as an ideal immigrant workforce. Indeed the interest in Mexican
> labor was so great that in some instances media characterized employers
> as fighting over Mexican labor: "Another Mexican war is on, and in the
> American Southwest again. But this time it is a fight for the Mexican, not
> against him; the prize of battle is the strength of his good right arm."[29]

The guest worker program created in 1917 was discontinued in 1924,
the same year as the formation of the U.S. Border Patrol.[30] This era also
saw the beginnings of what Flores describes as "narratives of the Mexican problem":

> Those participating in the narrative of the Mexican problem emphasized
> two main issues: (1) How to prevent future immigration?; and (2) What

to do with the Mexicans already living in the U.S.? . . . Civic leaders and regional planners engaged in rhetorical acts to create clearer borders between the U.S. and Mexico, between Americans and Mexicans, often relying on the strict enforcement of existing immigration laws.[31]

In 1929, unlawful entry into the United States became a misdemeanor and unlawful reentry became a felony.[32] For Mexicans, according to Flores, this law "dramatically change[d] the dynamics of immigration. Prior to the late 1920s, little regulation of Mexican immigration existed. Instead, Mexicans were often exempted from the enforcement of restrictionist policies, such as the head tax and the literacy laws."[33]

As unemployment worsened during the Great Depression, Mexicans were seen as "competition for jobs and a drain on social services."[34] Raids and deportations followed, as federal, state, and local governments engaged in a process of forced removal of about one million Mexicans throughout the 1930s.[35] This program is generally referred to as the Mexican "repatriation," but as scholars point out, the term "repatriation" is inaccurate: "Approximately 60 percent of the persons of Mexican ancestry removed to Mexico in the 1930s were U.S. citizens, many of them children who were effectively deported to Mexico when their immigrant parents were sent there."[36] Moreover, "hundreds of thousands more, wary of the changed climate, return[ed] to Mexico voluntarily."[37] The repatriation of the 1930s, as Kevin Johnson notes,

> violated the rights of persons of Mexican ancestry in almost too many ways to mention. Violations of the U.S. Constitution, as well as international law, are clear-cut. The Due Process, Equal Protection, and Fourth Amendment rights of persons stopped, detained, and deported from the United States were sacrificed. Through efforts to enforce the immigration laws, state and local governments also infringed on the federal immigration power.[38]

A sharp turnaround in policy occurred as a result of the labor shortages created by World War II, when the need for low-wage agricultural labor in the United States led to the establishment of the guest worker Bracero Program. The treaty establishing the program was negotiated in 1942 between the United States and Mexico, and endorsed by Congress in 1943 as Public Law 45. Under the Bracero Program, "Mexicans could live and work in the United States for up to nine months per year. The United States government nonetheless made it very clear that these imported workers could not displace domestic workers."[39] Shortly thereafter, railroad workers were recruited from Mexico under similar provisions.[40] "From 1948 to 1964," Mae Ngai observes, "the United States imported, on average, 200,000 braceros a year. Braceros worked in twenty-six states, the vast majority in California, Texas, and other southwestern states, and dominated crops such as cotton, citrus fruits, melons, lettuce, and truck vegetables."[41] The program "reached its height in 1959, when an unprecedented 450,000 Mexican migrant workers entered the United States."[42]

Unfortunately, when Braceros returned to Mexico, "they reported discrimination as well as substandard working and housing conditions."[43] Ngai observes that while data are incomplete, "available evidence suggests that workers registered upwards of several thousand formal complaints a year. . . . Underpayment was the most common cause for complaint. Others concerned housing, subsistence, illegal deductions, threats, mistreatment, and occupational risks."[44] As I recount elsewhere, "The program also began to face strong opposition from both domestic civil rights groups and the labor sector over the poor treatment of these workers by their domestic agricultural employers. Moreover, the Mexican government became dissatisfied with the United States upon hearing about abuses of civil and human rights."[45]

"Operation Wetback" was begun in the mid-1950s, even while the Bracero Program was still in place:

The United States established "Operation Wetback" to monitor the presence of Mexicans in the United States and deport any Mexican who resided unlawfully in the United States. This program occurred during a period of heightened fear of noncitizens. . . . "Operation Wetback" specifically targeted individuals of Mexican descent. During this massive campaign, the U.S. government deported over one million Mexican immigrants, U.S. citizens of Mexican ancestry, and, undoubtedly other Hispanic U.S. citizens.

Through "Operation Wetback," the United States treated individuals of Mexican ancestry similarly to the way it treated Mexican Americans during the repatriation of the 1930s. The Mexican American community was directly affected by this campaign because it was "aimed at racial groups, which meant that the burden of proving citizenship fell totally upon people of Mexican descent." Accordingly, those unable to present such proof were arrested and sent to Mexico. This hasty process of proving documentation infringed upon the rights of many Mexican Americans who were United States citizens or lawful permanent residents because some of them were unable to readily provide authorities with the documentation necessary to show their legal status in the United States.[46]

The so-called wetback problem of the 1950s was another powerful example of a rhetoric of hate, as described by Ngai:

> Critics associated "wetback" with "misery, disease, crime, and many other evils." . . .
>
> The construction of the "wetback" as a dangerous and criminal social pathogen fed the general racial stereotype "Mexican." A 1951 study . . . stated, "No careful distinctions are made between illegal aliens and local citizens of Mexican descent. They are lumped together as 'Mexicans' and the characteristics that are observed among the wetbacks are by extension assigned to the local people."[47]

Restrictions on immigration from Mexico continued in subsequent decades; the Immigration and Nationality Act of 1965 set strict quotas on the number of persons who could legally enter the United States from Latin American nations, and most Mexican migration to the United States in the 1960s and 1970s was temporary and short-term.[48]

The U.S. policy of bringing in a labor force from Mexico during times of high demand and sending them back to Mexico when the labor supply exceeded the demand paved a bumpy path for Mexicans aspiring to become U.S. citizens. Mexicans who arrived as guest workers established ties in the United States, and many of them economically benefited from the low wages they earned because of the high rate of exchange between the U.S. dollar and Mexican peso.[49] This economic benefit, coupled with the establishment of families, gave many Mexicans an incentive to remain in the United States beyond the time permitted by the U.S. government.[50] Some Mexicans returned to Mexico and eventually made or tried to make their way back into the United States by crossing the U.S.-Mexico border, while others remained in the United States, risking removal by deportation or repatriation.[51]

The Mexican Narratives: From *Bandido* to Peon to Contagion

A number of scholars have analyzed the imagery and narratives associated with Mexicans in the United States. The earliest stereotype is the Mexican *bandido*, which, as Steven Bender notes in *Running for the Border*, "dates from the mid-nineteenth century, during which time cattle rustling, horse thievery, and other border banditry were rampant in the upheaval that followed the loss of considerable Mexican territory to the United States and the subsequent struggles for control of Mexico's government. Cavalries, posses, and the notorious Texas Rangers routinely pursued bandits into Mexico."[52] Not surprisingly, however,

> Media imagery of Mexicans running south for the Mexican border as desperados with the law in pursuit does not fully match history's lessons. The realities of U.S.-Mexico border crossings to escape authorities extend to other groups in addition to Mexicans. Moreover, . . . some of the crossings by Mexicans were prompted by circumstances much different from the familiar media images of the marauding, heartless bandido driven by depraved greed and bloodthirsty savagery.[53]

Lisa Flores observes that during the early part of the twentieth century, when Mexican immigrants were welcomed, Mexicans were characterized as hardworking and easily controlled peons. According to what she calls the "narrative of need,"

> Mexicans were ideal because they constituted a controllable workforce suited to the particular demands of agricultural labor. That Mexicans constituted peon labor served at least two goals in this narrative. First, peon labor was defined as poor, uneducated, and without ambition. Peon came to signify an interest in day-to-day life over a desire to get ahead. . . . This perceived lack of ambition in Mexicans made them, in this narrative, particularly well suited to temporary labor, such as that needed in agriculture. . . . Further, unlike other undesirable populations, Mexicans were unlikely to save enough money either to move into semi-skilled positions or to be able to buy land or other permanent residences in the U.S.[54]

Yet, after economic downturns in the United States resulting from the 1929 stock market crash and the ensuing Great Depression, a counternarrative arose that Flores describes as the narrative of "the Mexican problem":

> The common descriptors of Mexicans shifted from docile to diseased and criminal. The mainstream American presses of the late 1920s and early 1930s were filled with commentaries on the pervasiveness of social contagions. Tales of Mexicans with illness appeared, and the Mexican threat was depicted as both numerical and visceral. . . . These undesirable immigrants were invested with social powers of change; they threatened racial purity and superiority.[55]

High-level government officials contributed to the rhetoric about the threats posed by Mexicans and their supposed criminality:

> U.S. Secretary of Labor William N. Doak . . . easily equated many types of immigration with criminality, [and] asserted in the public press that

immigrants were responsible for many of the nation's dilemmas, including crime, communism, drug activity, and unemployment. This was not an atypical argument; it was voiced by many others.[56]

The historian Mae Ngai also discusses the importance of these narrative shifts in her powerful book *Impossible Subjects: Illegal Aliens and the Making of Modern America*:

> The racial formations of Asians and Mexicans in the 1920s were particularly significant because they modified a racial map of a nation that had been marked principally by the contours of white and black. . . .
>
> During the 1920s the legal traditions that had justified racial discrimination against African Americans were extended to other ethno-racial groups in immigration law through the use of euphemism ("aliens ineligible to citizenship") and the invention of new categories of identity ("national origins").[57]

As discussed in chapter 2, echoes of these narrative shifts continue today in rhetoric that associates Mexican immigrants with a population explosion, a cultural takeover, crime waves, and job losses for U.S. citizens. And once again, negative portrayals of immigrants coincide with harsh anti-immigrant laws geared toward an enforcement-only approach. Arguably the most recent cycle of anti-immigrant rhetoric and legislation began in the aftermath of the terrorist attacks of September 11, 2001, which resulted in renewed fear of foreigners. Despite legislative proposals for comprehensive immigration reform in 2005, 2006, and 2007, the bills that have actually been passed have focused only on harsher enforcement measures, rather than the truly comprehensive reform that is necessary.[58] The only other significant immigration legislation largely focused on narrower issues, such as the passage of the DREAM Act. After a decade of legislative efforts, the DREAM Act was narrowly defeated in 2010. Only time will tell if other forms of immigration reform will be passed in the near future. The last chapter of this book will examine the prospects for the passage of either form of legislation.

6

Sociological and Psychological Insights on Anti-Immigrant Bias

I am troubled by the demonization of immigrants, legal or
illegal, in our party. We've got a country that was built on
immigrants and immigration, and we've kind of lost sight of
that.
—Rep. Blake Farenthold (R–TX), August 1, 2011

Anti-immigrant discourse, ranging from factually incorrect assertions
to inflammatory rhetoric, has a significant impact on public perceptions
and the implementation of public policy. As we have seen in chapter 2,
there are well known cases in which those who make offensively anti-
black or misogynistic comments face strong public condemnation. For
example, in 2007 Don Imus was fired from his radio talk show after
his disgusting slur against the Rutgers women's basketball team. In 2012
there was a national outcry against Rush Limbaugh for his sexist insults
of a law student, Sandra Fluke, who had testified before Congress concerning contraception. Limbaugh's radio show lost dozens of sponsors
as a result.[1] Such outcry almost never occurs when public figures make
anti-Latino and anti-immigrant comments, as we saw in the case of Katt
Williams, who suffered no negative consequences for his racist comments, and in fact was rewarded with a comedy special on Showtime.
Sadly, it thus seems that anti-immigrant attacks have become part of the
American collective psyche.

This chapter will provide a brief overview of insights from media
studies scholars, psychologists, and other social scientists that can help

explain why anti-immigrant attitudes persist, why they are considered acceptable, and how they affect public policy.

Implicit Bias and Stereotyping

As one scholar has observed, "Psychologists have long recognized that we do not enter the perceptual arena empty-handed but, rather, with what is sometimes referred to as perceptual baggage. Perceptual baggage includes our unique idiosyncratic collection of experience, needs, and desires as well as more common, culturally shared beliefs."[2] This is relevant for our study because biases and negative stereotypes about immigrants have become part of the shared beliefs of the culture as a whole.

The American Values Institute, an antiracist scholarly consortium, provides a useful definition of implicit bias:

> Also known as Hidden Bias or Unconscious Bias, Implicit Bias arose conceptually as a way to explain why discrimination persists, even though polling and other research clearly shows that people oppose it. . . .
>
> In 1995, Doctors Anthony Greenwald and M. R. Benaji posited that it was possible that our social behavior was not completely under our conscious control. In *Implicit Social Cognition: Attitudes, Self-Esteem and Stereotypes,* Greenwald and Benaji argued that much of our social behavior is driven by learned stereotypes that operate automatically—and therefore unconsciously—when we interact with other people.[3]

To understand implicit bias, we also need to understand the concept of schemas, "templates of knowledge that help us organize specific examples into broader categories," as explained by the UCLA law professor Jerry Kang:

> When we see, for example, something with a flat seat, a back, and some legs, we recognize it as a "chair." Regardless of whether it is plush or wooden, with wheels or bolted down, we know what to do with an object that fits into the category "chair." . . . We have schemas not only for

objects, but also processes, such as how to order food at a restaurant. . . . [U]nless something goes wrong, these thoughts take place automatically without our awareness or conscious direction. In this way, most cognitions are implicit. . . .

What is interesting is that schemas apply not only to objects (e.g., "chairs") or behaviors (e.g., "ordering food") but also to human beings (e.g., "the elderly"). We naturally assign people into various social categories divided by salient and chronically accessible traits, such as age, gender, race, and role. And just as we might have implicit cognitions that help us walk and drive, we have implicit social cognitions that guide our thinking about social categories. . . .

If we unpack these schemas further, we see that some of the underlying cognition includes stereotypes, which are simply traits that we associate with a category. For instance, if we think that a particular category of human beings is frail—such as the elderly—we will not raise our guard. If we think that another category is foreign—such as Asians—we will be surprised by their fluent English. These cognitions also include attitudes, which are overall, evaluative feelings that are positive or negative. . . .

Though our shorthand schemas of people may be helpful in some situations, they also can lead to discriminatory behaviors if we are not careful. Given the critical importance of exercising fairness and equality in the court system, lawyers, judges, jurors, and staff should be particularly concerned about identifying such possibilities. Do we, for instance, associate aggressiveness with Black men, such that we see them as more likely to have started the fight than to have responded in self-defense? Or have we already internalized the lessons of Martin Luther King, Jr. and navigate life in a perfectly "colorblind" (or gender-blind, ethnicity-blind, class-blind, etc.) way?[4]

Forming Attitudes: Stigma and Contagions

Studies on the impact of stigma are also useful in understanding how anti-immigrant rhetoric affects immigrants as well as other individuals who are marked as "foreign," including Latino and Latina U.S. citizens and legal residents. In his groundbreaking book *Stigma: Notes on the Management of Spoiled Identity*, Erving Goffman observed that

> By definition, . . . we believe the person with a stigma is not quite human. On this assumption we exercise varieties of discriminatory practices, through which we effectively, if often unthinkingly, reduce his life chances. We construct a stigma-theory, an ideology to explain his inferiority and account for the danger he represents, sometimes rationalizing an animosity based on other differences, such as those of social class.[5]

Researchers have written about stigma in a variety of contexts. They note that the person who is stigmatized "is viewed as different, with this difference involving important qualities that set the possessor off as deviant, flawed, spoiled, or undesirable."[6] "Much like contagions, stigmas have real and lasting physiological and psychological effects that taint the subject of the stigma with lasting moral repugnance."[7] As the scholars Howard Kunreuther and Paul Slovic observe, "When we think of the prime targets for stigmatization in our society, members of minority groups, the aged, homosexuals, drug addicts, and persons afflicted with physical deformities and mental disabilities, we can appreciate the affect-laden images that, rightly or wrongly, are associated with such individuals."[8] Of particular relevance for our discussion is the role of the news media: "the greatest contributor to stigma, by far, is the news media."[9]

The Influence of Media: The Dominant Gaze

The study of media portrayals and their impact on racial perceptions is not new in the social sciences. In a 1977 report, the U.S. Civil Rights Commission drew a connection between stereotypical portrayals of racial and ethnic minorities on television and the "beliefs, attitudes, and behavior" of the viewing public.[10] The study concluded that these media stereotypes had a distinct impact on race relations in American society:

for example, "40 percent of white children questioned attributed their knowledge of how they believed blacks looked, talked, and dressed to what they saw on television."[11] In 1993 another commission report concluded that "news media has tremendous influence on the attitudes of viewers and readers regarding race relations in this country."[12]

In her groundbreaking 1991 article "Race and the Dominant Gaze: Narratives of Law and Inequality in Popular Film," Margaret Russell argues that racist portrayals, such as the one in the film *Birth of a Nation,* exemplify what she called the "dominant gaze," that is,

> the tendency of mainstream culture to replicate, through narrative and imagery, racial inequalities and biases which exist throughout society. I derive the term "dominant gaze" from Laura Mulvey's feminist critique of Hollywood movies, "Visual Pleasure and Narrative Cinema," in which she contends that popular film essentially serves the political function of subjugating female bodies and experiences to the interpretation and control of a heterosexual "male gaze." . . .
>
> Extending Mulvey's metaphor, I use the term "dominant gaze" to describe the tendency of American popular cinema to objectify and trivialize the racial identity and experiences of people of color, even when it purports to represent them. Like Mulvey's male gaze, the dominant gaze subtly invites the viewer to empathize and identify with its viewpoint as natural, universal, and beyond challenge; it marginalizes other perspectives to bolster its own legitimacy in defining narratives and images. . . . [T]he dominant gaze's power lies in projecting stereotypes and biases as essential "truths."[13]

Russell's work is of course still relevant today and very applicable to the rhetoric produced by the anti-immigrant lobby, which shapes societal perceptions of immigration, immigrants, and the Latina/Latino community in general.

In a 1994 study, three researchers at the University of Western Ontario examined the formation of attitudes toward new immigrant groups. They observe that indirect information may be especially important in the formation of attitudes toward new immigrant groups because individuals often have no personal information on which to base their attitudes toward such groups. Thus, information about these groups comes from a variety of other sources (e.g., news media, surveys, acquaintances). . . .

[Accordingly], initial information might be the most important information that people receive. This would suggest that the media should be especially sensitive to its portrayal of new immigrant groups.[14]

In a later study, these same researchers pointed out that the media have a consequential impact on those who have not decided on their positions with respect to a particular group. The study found that "people who hold ambivalent attitudes toward a group are more likely to systematically process persuasive messages about that group than are people who hold non-ambivalent attitudes toward the particular group."[15]

However, as we have seen throughout this book, the media and others repeatedly portray undocumented immigrants as criminals, as people determined to take jobs from citizens, or as frightening hordes seeking somehow to invade and overthrow this country. Moreover, as I argued in an earlier article, even when contemporary media portrayals of Latinos and Latinas are repackaged with ostensibly positive titles such as the "Latin Explosion" or "Latin Boom," these are nothing more than new ways to objectify and commodify a community using classic stereotypes.[16]

Transference and Displacement

Legal scholars have repeatedly noted that recent incarnations of immigration debates have racial overtones, yet these observations go either unread or largely disregarded by the national media. Indeed, in a nationwide poll, "when asked what fuels the current anti-immigrant sentiment in the United States, 64 percent of Hispanics in the poll mentioned one factor: 'racism against immigrants from Latin America.'"[17] As the leading immigration scholar Kevin Johnson argues, "the harsh treatment of *noncitizens* reveals just how this society views *citizens* of color" (emphasis in original).[18] In his 1998 article "Race, the Immigration Laws, and Domestic Race Relations," Johnson looks to the psychological theories of transference and displacement to help explain why immigrants of color are "society's scapegoats":

> Psychological theory at times has served as a tool for analyzing the legal implications of racial discrimination. In some ways, the reaction to immigrants of color can be explained by the psychological construct known as transference "in which feelings toward one person are refocused on another." Transference ordinarily occurs unconsciously in the individual. The general public, in light of modern sensibilities, often is foreclosed from directly attacking minority citizens, at least publicly. Society can, however, lash out with full force at noncitizens of color. In so doing, they contend that the attacks are not racially motivated but that other facially neutral factors animate restrictionist goals. Such attacks amount to transference of frustration from domestic minorities to immigrants of color.
>
> The related psychological construct of displacement also helps us understand the phenomenon. "Displacement" is "[a] defense mechanism in which a drive or feeling is shifted upon a substitute object, one that is psychologically more available. For example, aggressive impulses may be displaced, as in 'scapegoating,' upon people (or even inanimate objects) *who are not sources of frustration but are safer to attack.*"
>
> Psychological studies show how displaced frustration may unconsciously result in the development of racial prejudice. For example, one famous study of displaced aggression found that negative attitudes toward persons of Japanese and Mexican ancestry increased after a tedious testing session that caused children to miss a trip to the movies. Animosity was displaced from the test-givers, immune from attack because of their positions of authority, to defenseless racial minorities.
>
> Such examples square with the history of scapegoating immigrants for the social problems of the day. For example, the U.S. economy went south in the late 1800s and the frustration was displaced from diffuse economic causes to Chinese immigrants. Gordon Allport offered a most

apt example: "Most Germans did not see the connection between their humiliating defeat in World War I and their subsequent anti-Semitism." Frustration was displaced from complex real-world causes to a simple— and defenseless—solution.[19]

Stereotyping and stigma have a significant impact on public policy. Negative attitudes make it easier for a society to create policies targeting those who are stigmatized. There is ample evidence of this in U.S. domestic jurisprudence relating to immigrant groups, including the national origin quota system and the establishment of "whiteness" as a prerequisite for naturalization, which effectively excluded Asian immigrants from the United States. Later examples included the internment of Japanese immigrants and Japanese Americans, regardless of their citizenship, during World War II; the refusal to accept many European Jewish refugees fleeing the Holocaust; and the 1950s "Operation Wetback" campaign resulting in mass deportations of people of Mexican ancestry. The Immigration Act of 1965 imposed draconian limits on migration from the Western Hemisphere.[20] Unfortunately, the current anti-immigrant climate could well result in a new wave of punitive policies unless rational alternatives are found.

7

A Pragmatic Proposal for Immigration Reform

We need immigration reform that will secure our borders, and . . . that finally brings the 12 million people who are here illegally out of the shadows. . . . We must assert our values and reconcile our principles as a nation of immigrants and a nation of laws.
—President Barack Obama, June 28, 2008

Toning Down the Rhetoric

The *War of the Worlds* radio broadcast discussed in the introduction was a hoax concerning a Martian invasion. The stunt made Orson Wells famous and caused a short-term panic across the country. Nearly a hundred years later, that broadcast exemplifies the media's ability to create and even distort reality. In many respects, the hyperbolic radio broadcast about Martian invaders parallels today's vitriolic attacks against immigrant workers.[1] Perhaps the recent incarnations of the *War of the Worlds* broadcast will bring fame to alarmists like Tom Tancredo and Lou Dobbs, but history will likely portray this era as more akin to the McCarthy-led witch hunts of the past.

Thus far the alarmists have made a considerable impact on the national and local stage. Too many non-Latino Americans believe that we are in the midst of an invasion that will engulf the country in a crime wave and lead to economic ruin for innocent, law-abiding U.S. citizens. With too few exceptions, conservative leaders have joined the anti-immigrant bandwagon, and leaders in the Democratic Party have failed to stand up to the hateful rhetoric.[2] Deportations rates during the Obama administration, in fact, are higher than those in any previous administration.

We need to end the hostile rhetoric aimed at undocumented immigrants. Immigration policy must be based on reality, not hateful hyperbole. More scholars, advocates, reasoned media members, and political leaders need to examine the facts and speak out.[3] Be they Democrats or Republicans, those in favor of sound immigration policy should place their votes with candidates who actually support such policies. Only one 2012 Republican presidential candidate—Governor Rick Perry—had advocated an economically sound border policy, and he very likely lost the nomination in part because of that policy.

Some politicians have taken important steps toward standing up to the xenophobic attacks and the inhumane discourse against Latino and Latina immigrants.[4] In his last State of the Union address, George W. Bush called for a change in the rhetoric concerning immigration and pleaded for reasoned approaches toward the challenges facing America:

> We also need to acknowledge that we will never fully secure our border until we create a lawful way for foreign workers to come here and support our economy. . . . This will take pressure off the border and allow law enforcement to concentrate on those who mean us harm. We must also find a sensible and humane way to deal with people here illegally. Illegal immigration is complicated, but it can be resolved. And it must be resolved in a way that upholds both our laws and our highest ideals.[5]

As Barack Obama stated when he was still a senator, "for reform to work, we must also respond to what pulls people to America. Where we can reunite families, we should. Where we can bring in more foreign born workers with the skills our economy needs, we should."[6] Then-Senator Hilary Clinton noted that she favored "a path to earned legalization to undocumented immigrants who are willing to work hard, play by the rules, learn English and pay fines."[7]

During his first term in office, President Obama repeatedly stated that he could do little to pass comprehensive immigration reform or the DREAM Act without congressional action. But by 2012, it seemed that the discourse was at least starting to change. In January 2012, in the midst of the Republican presidential primaries, the former Florida governor Jeb Bush warned his party of the consequences of taking anti-immigrant stances and its effect on the Latino and Latina electorate.[8] Moreover, an up-and-coming young Latino (or Hispanic, as he would likely describe himself) Republican took the prospect of the election to advance a more reasonable dialogue. While his party's leader of the moment, Mitt Romney, promoted a policy of self-deportation—making life so miserable for the undocumented that they would deport themselves—U.S. Senator Marco Rubio, a party darling and likely candidate for the 2016 presidential race, took a politically savvy but somewhat dangerous approach and courageously called for reasoned debate. Such an effort, no matter the political motivations behind it, took considerable courage. And while I have often been critical of the good senator, much credit should be given to him for helping to change the tenor of immigration discourse. His efforts were not only wise advice for his party, they may make it much more difficult for the hatemongering to continue. During his speech at the 2012 Hispanic Leadership Network conference, Rubio observed,

> For those of us who come from the conservative movement, we must admit that there are those among us who have used rhetoric that is harsh and intolerable, inexcusable, and we must admit, myself included, that sometimes we've been too slow in condemning that language for what it is.

In another part of the speech, Rubio expressed sympathy for the plight of DREAMers:

> there is broad support in America for the notion that for those children that were brought here at a very young age, by their parents through no

fault of their own, who have grown up here their entire lives, and now want to serve in the military or are high academic achievers and want to go to school and contribute to America's future, I think there is broad bipartisan support for the notion that we should somehow figure out a way to accommodate them.[9]

In June 2012, the Obama administration announced that the president would use his executive authority to implement the Deferred Action for Childhood Arrivals (DACA) program. DACA is part of a plan that would allow undocumented youth (those individuals who would have benefited from the DREAM Act) to halt deportation proceedings against them, or if not in proceedings, allow these undocumented youth to seek permission to remain in the United States for two years and apply for employment authorization. While many critics, perhaps correctly, viewed this effort as a ploy to garner support from the Latino/a electorate, the president set forth a narrative that was far different from so many other statements on undocumented immigrants:

> As I said in my speech on the economy yesterday, it makes no sense to expel talented young people, who, for all intents and purposes, are Americans—they've been raised as Americans; understand themselves to be part of this country—to expel these young people who want to staff our labs, or start new businesses, or defend our country simply because of the actions of their parents—or because of the inaction of politicians.
>
> Put yourself in their shoes. Imagine you've done everything right your entire life—studied hard, worked hard, maybe even graduated at the top of your class—only to suddenly face the threat of deportation to a country that you know nothing about, with a language that you may not even speak.
>
> That's what gave rise to the DREAM Act. It says that if your parents brought you here as a child, if you've been here for five years, and you're willing to go to college or serve in our military, you can one day earn your citizenship. And I have said time and time and time again to Congress that, send me the DREAM Act, put it on my desk, and I will sign it right away.[10]

Thus, politicians from very different political perspectives have begun to change the undocumented immigration discourse. Therefore, a key strategy for changing the negative images that reach the public concerning undocumented immigration may be to confront the hate and to begin to educate the media, the public, and the regulatory community about the effects their messages may cause. Accordingly, challenges to negative media portrayals of immigrants should not be limited to academic publications such as this one.

Even if the media and political leaders refuse to change their rhetoric due to inertia, stubbornness, or genuine philosophical differences, they now have a more pragmatic motivation to change.[11] According to the latest U.S. census figures, there are 52 million Latinos/Latinas in the United States, constituting 16.7 percent of the population.[12] Although only about 24 million Latinos are currently eligible to vote, that number is estimated to double by 2030.[13] Despite its diversity, this group has considerable political and economic power, and its members are becoming increasingly politically active.[14] At least one scholar has observed that as a result of changing demographics, former minority groups may one day use their political power to shift the pendulum of immigration policy in their favor.[15]

Continuing anti-immigrant rhetoric is unquestionably filled with considerable risk. Indeed, reports and polls do suggest a backlash against baseless anti-immigrant attacks.[16] For instance, George W. Bush "won 44 percent of the Hispanic vote in 2004, but Republican Congressional candidates received only 29 percent in 2006, according to exit polls. A [2007] Gallop Poll showed that only 11 percent [of Latinos and Latinas] now identify as Republicans."[17] According to the Pew Research Center, "the gap between Latinos identifying themselves as Democrats and Republicans jumped 13 percentage points, giving Democrats a 34-point advantage."[18] The Pew Hispanic Center notes that in the 2012 presidential election, "Latinos voted for President Barack Obama over Republican Mitt Romney by 71% to 27%."[19] Simon Rosenberg, president of the New Democrat Network, argued that "Republicans should be terrified [because] [t]he positions most of their candidates are taking now will

make it very difficult for them to win the presidency."²⁰ The journalist
Fred Barnes noted that "by dwelling, often emotionally, on the problem
of illegal immigration as a paramount issue and as if nothing is being
done to deal with it, Republicans are alienating Hispanic Americans, the
fastest growing voting bloc in the country."²¹

Indeed, a 2013 poll provides interesting insights on Latino engagement in the electoral process:

> A new Latino Decisions poll finds that Latino voters are paying very close
> attention to the immigration debate in Congress and that a candidate's
> stance on immigration policy will directly effect how many Latino votes
> they win or lose. The new poll of 800 Latino registered voters nation-
> wide, . . . conducted in partnership with America's Voice, SEIU, and the
> National Council of La Raza, . . . [found that] 58% of Latino voters now
> rate immigration reform as the most important issue they want Congress
> and the President to address, up from 35% who rated immigration reform
> as the top concern in our November 2012 election eve poll. The economy
> and jobs was rated second at 38% followed by health care (19%) and edu-
> cation (15%). . . . Not only are Latino voters paying attention, but they
> expect Congress to act on comprehensive immigration reform this year.
> 74% said it was extremely or very important that Congress pass immigra-
> tion reform in 2013.²²

For reform to actually occur, the Latino/Latina community must continue to use its significant economic and political power to insist upon
effective immigration reform and an end to the targeting of undocumented immigrants, documented immigrants, and all others who may
be perceived as immigrants, which of course would include Latinos as
well as other ethnic and racial minority groups. The community needs
to flex its muscle at the polls and reject any candidate who refuses to end
the hateful lies against immigrants and the Latino community.

As the columnist Andres Oppenheimer has argued, national Latino
civil rights groups such as La Raza should launch a nationwide "Ya
Basta" campaign against those who bash Latino and Latina immigrants.²³

I would argue further that the Latino and Latina community, and like-minded informed groups, also need to state loud and clear that those who engage in such rhetoric will pay at the polls for their actions; those who stand by and do little to support these communities will equally pay for their failure to act. And, as Senator John McCain has recently stated, *"If we continue to polarize the Latino/Hispanic vote our chances for being in the majority are minimal. This issue of illegal immigration has obviously been a major driving factor in the decision making of the Hispanic voter."*[24]

This transformative political effort must be ongoing, and must be undertaken with the zeal displayed by the young student activist DREAMers. They have not only become the face of immigration reform, they helped change the tenor of the debate concerning the DREAM Act. Such zeal and resulting change must be expanded upon to apply to the broader issue of comprehensive reform.[25] Not unlike the legal scholars who have called for coalitional movements and for reformulations of identity politics with labels such as political race,[26] Latinos and Latinas should seek alliances with like-minded people of color and whites, business leaders, and civic leaders to create a counternarrative not only in the media, but also in this country's collective psyche.[27] Such a strategy is not unlike the grassroots efforts several years ago by immigrant groups opposing the House of Representatives' proposed H.R. 4437, the Border Protection, Antiterrorism, and Illegal Immigration Control Act of 2005. Though this effort may have led to the talk radio backlash discussed earlier, which perhaps led to the ultimate passage of the restrictive, enforcement-focused Secure Fence Act, H.R. 6061, the protests in over a hundred U.S. cities by over a million Americans should not be forgotten. Instead of shying away from modern-day bullies and ignorant cowards, advocates of an inclusive and productive America should remember April 10, 2006, not as a day of ethnic divisiveness (as the nativists would have us believe), but as a day of recognition of the value of immigrants and diversity.[28]

One can hope that as a result of informational campaigns to fight disinformation, rhetoric, and fearmongering, people will become better informed about the economic benefits conferred by undocumented workers; will vote for reforms that assist and not punish states that have economies that attract immigrants; will support economically sound and humane immigration policy; and will no longer be persuaded by claims that America is about to be overridden and changed irrevocably by dark-skinned, criminally inclined, poverty-stricken hordes. But perhaps an equally important factor in changing people's minds about immigration will be their firsthand experience of the negative economic consequences of state- and local-level anti-immigration policies, such as those in Arizona and Alabama (see chapter 4).

The Three Policy Alternatives: Deportation, Amnesty, and a Guest Worker Program

Before the discussion of my proposal for comprehensive immigration reform, I will address the three policy options that are usually discussed in this context: (1) mass deportation; (2) blanket amnesty, with no attempt to increase the responsibility of the businesses that hire undocumented workers; and (3) a guest worker program.

Mass Deportation

Once again the nonprofit, nonpartisan organization ProCon.org is a good source of interesting quotes on the issue of deportation. Jim Gilchrist of the Minuteman Project exemplifies the alarmist position:

> I'm pro-deportation or if you want to use a nicer word, pro-repatriation. You cannot have a defeatist attitude towards the problem and have a solution. The repatriation of illegals must begin with a recognition of the problem and a plan. We may be called names, but the names our grandchildren will call us will be worse when they have to live in a destroyed country. There must be a multi-faceted approach, including arresting illegals and also cutting off social welfare programs to them.[29]

All reasonable sources, however, conclude that mass deportation is unsound economic policy, is simply too expensive, and will not put an end to undocumented immigration, especially if domestic capital continues its demands for undocumented labor. Domestic business sectors such as the agricultural, construction, and service industries are never acknowledged as creating this demand, and ironically are somehow seen as victims in this century-long struggle.[30]

Referring to the "false allure" of mass deportation, a Center for American Progress report concluded that the "costs of a massive deportation policy would not only be substantial, but in many ways, financially reckless. Implementing such a policy would seriously jeopardize our commitment to secure the homeland and pay for our commitments overseas, as well as threaten other vital national priorities."[31] As a *New York Times* editorial put it, "The enforcement-only approach—building a 700-mile wall and engaging in a campaign of mass deportation and harassment to rip 12 million people from the national fabric—would be an impossible waste of time and resources. It would destroy families and weaken the economy."[32]

Interestingly, a number of prominent Republicans have also publicly voiced opposition to a policy of deportation. One example is Tom Ridge, former secretary of homeland security:

> The debate we are engaged in presently is a good and necessary one. However, a solution based solely on enforcement is not. . . . The current flow of illegal immigrants and visa overstayers has made it extremely difficult for our border and interior enforcement agencies. . . . Despite a record performance on deportations from ICE [U.S. Immigration and Customs Enforcement] the past two years, at current rates it would take nearly 70 years to deport all of the estimated 11 million people living here illegally, even if not a single new illegal alien entered our territory. Attempting to deport everybody is neither feasible nor wise.[33]

John McCain made this statement on the Senate floor:

I have listened to and understand the concerns of those who simply advocate sealing our borders and rounding up and deporting undocumented
workers currently in residence here. But that's easier said than done. . . . I
have yet to hear a single proponent of this point of view offer one realistic proposal for locating, apprehending, and returning to their countries
of origin over 11 million people. How do we do that? . . . it would take
200,000 buses extending along a 1700 mile long line to deport 11 million
people. That's assuming we had the resources to locate and apprehend
all 11 million, or even half that number, which we don't have and, we all
know, won't ever have.[34]

Many individuals and organizations have pointed out the personal
toll inflicted on families by zealous deportation policies. The interfaith
New Sanctuary Movement, calling for a moratorium on deportation
raids, has stated, "We are deeply grieved by the violence done to families
through immigration raids. We cannot in good conscience ignore such
suffering and injustice."[35] The independent media coalition Indy Bay has
called for a "Child Citizen Protection Act":

Deportation destroys families and leaves U.S. citizen children without
parents. Over 1 in 10 families are mixed status: at least 1 parent is a non-
citizen, and 1 child a citizen. We now have a vehicle to help protect our
U.S. citizen children from the devastating effects of deportation: The
Child Citizen Protection Act . . . would allow an immigration judge to
consider the best interest of U.S. citizen children before deporting their
parent.[36]

The advocacy group Families for Freedom also points out the inhu-
maneness of deportation:

Every year, nearly 200,000 non-citizens—many with kids who are U.S.
citizens—are deported and torn away from their families . . . resulting in
more single parent households and psychological and financial hardship,
or forcing their U.S. citizen children into deportation with them. These

American children may have to start over in a country with a new language, fewer resources and an uncertain future. America's immigration laws force American children to lose their parent or their country. Mandatory deportation is a life sentence of exile. Such a severe "one size fits all" punishment cannot be the basis of our immigration system.[37]

Amnesty

On the other side of the spectrum from mass deportation is amnesty, or perhaps more appropriately referred to as a path toward legalization or citizenship, a reform process that would lead to legalization for currently undocumented immigrants. This option is widely considered a much more liberal-minded and pro-immigrant approach. There is understandably a certain amount of disagreement, however, over the use of the term. The American Friends Service Committee has explained the difference between the terms "legalization" and "amnesty" as follows:

> Most people—immigrants, advocates, and policy makers—refer to the measures adopted in 1986 as an "amnesty." . . . In the years since the passage of The Immigration Reform and Control Act of 1986 (IRCA), the word "amnesty" has become a political hot potato—tossed around by proponents and opponents of the concept in order to label the other side.
>
> Immigrants and advocates who support amnesty are of two minds about the term "amnesty." Some say that "amnesty" means extending LPR [legal permanent residency status] to undocumented immigrants. . . . Within the immigrants' rights community, others argue that, although they also support granting LPR status to undocumented immigrants, legislators in Congress are unwilling to even begin a conversation if the term "amnesty" is used. Therefore, they prefer the term "legalization." Some would also say that there is a substantive difference between the concepts of "legalization" and "amnesty," in that legalization would include a more stringent application process or other provisions, including measures to regulate future flows of migration. At the same time, however, others

would argue that the concepts are exactly the same; the difference is simply the term. Proponents of the term "legalization" argue that "amnesty" implies "forgiveness" for a "crime." Immigration, they believe, should not be seen as a crime. Proponents of the term "amnesty" say that no human being is illegal, and so they do not need to ask for "legalization." "Amnesty," they believe, is the more appropriate term, because it asks forgiveness for breaking a law, albeit an unjust law. Amnesty International, for example, has been using the term for years, but it does not cast political prisoners in a negative light. And so, the debate continues.[38]

Except for Rick Perry, none of the candidates for the 2012 Republican presidential nomination took anything resembling a pro-amnesty or pro-legalization stance. ProCon.org again provides a representative sampling of anti-amnesty rhetoric from Republican legislators: "Amnesty is bad policy and sends the message that immigrants are better off breaking our laws rather than respecting them" (Randy Neugebauer, R-TX). "Amnesty and a path to citizenship . . . would be a slap in the face to all those who have followed the law and have come to America legally" (James Sensenbrenner, R-WI). "Americans are not interested in rewarding illegal aliens with a $2.5 trillion blanket amnesty" (Tom Tancredo, R-CO). "Amnesty for lawbreakers is not the answer, and it's time to rethink birthright citizenship" (Ron Paul, R-TX).[39]

In contrast, Democratic politicians and labor unions were among the proponents of amnesty the last time it was being seriously considered in Congress. Senator John Kerry "supported and was prepared to vote for amnesty from 1986. And it is essential to have immigration reform. Anyone who has been in this country for five or six years, who's paid their taxes, who has stayed out of trouble, ought to be able to translate into an American citizenship immediately, not waiting."[40] The AFL-CIO released a number of supportive statements, including the following 2005 letter from its president, John J. Sweeney:

Senators McCain and Kennedy introduced a comprehensive immigration reform bill that will provide a path to legal status to the 12 million people who have been working hard, paying their taxes and contributing to their communities. We are strongly supportive of the concept of legalization, recognizing that raising the floor for undocumented workers and bringing them out of the shadows will improve working conditions for all workers. We are also in agreement that if this bill moves forward, we will seek to expand its labor protections considerably to ensure a positive outcome for all workers.[41]

It seems that despite the support for a form of legalization from many interest groups and political leaders, the attempt to successfully pass immigration reform providing for legalization is simply unlikely in the current political climate.

A Guest Worker Program

An intermediate step between legalization and an enforcement-first approach is a guest worker program. In an effort to address both the undocumented immigration debate and the domestic need for labor in agriculture and service-related industries, President George W. Bush called for a "new temporary worker program to match willing foreign workers with willing U.S. employers" to fill jobs that Americans did not want.[42] Under the president's proposal, "the federal government [would] offer temporary worker status to undocumented men and women now employed in the United States and to those in foreign countries who have been offered employment in the United States. The workers under temporary status must . . . return home after their period of work expires."[43]

Pro-immigrant advocates and scholars have also called for guest worker programs that would provide jobs and protect undocumented immigrants from the many types of exploitation that occurred during the Bracero Program in the mid-twentieth century (see chapter 5). In *Deporting Our Souls: Values, Morality, and Immigration Policy,* Bill Ong Hing wrote,

Humanizing guestworkers rather than commodifying them helps us understand why providing them with a path to legalization is probably the right thing to do. . . . [A]s enfranchised, potential citizens (with human faces), guestworkers would less likely be subordinated and more likely be treated with respect.[44]

All of society would benefit from a guest worker program. The country's antiterrorism resources would not be wasted on arrests of low-income farm workers. Interested business sectors would not have to waste funds and energy playing shell games with their workers and the government. Increased efficiencies and productivity would assist everyone, including domestic citizens, especially in terms of the cost of food and greater efficiency and benefits from effective law enforcement.

Crucially, an effective guest worker program would enable states to collect accurate data on their guest workers and immigration flows; the data can be used to call upon the federal government to pay its fair share of the additional costs borne by the various states' education and healthcare industries. In many respects, under the current system, the federal government is also a free rider in terms of undocumented immigration. As attested by the numerous studies addressed in chapter 3, undocumented immigrants create real and ongoing benefits to our federal government.

An effective guest worker program could also undermine the hateful rhetoric that permeates the undocumented immigration debate. Honest, hardworking people will no longer bear the stigma of being "illegal." Domestic business sectors will have to provide basic rights and opportunities in return for a willing labor force that will come out of the shadows and finally be treated as human beings, as true guests, not part of any so-called invasion or threat to our cultural and political fabric.

The following pages will provide a starting point toward reform, or at least a starting point toward honest debate that can address reform and assist all affected by our current immigration policy. The following section will incorporate liberal legalization components and more moderate guest worker proposals, and seek to hold domestic business sectors accountable as well as assist state and local governments disproportionately affected by our current domestic immigration priorities.

The 2013 Kennedy-Bell Comprehensive Immigration Reform Law

The proposal advocated here, which I have dubbed the 2013 Kennedy-Bell Comprehensive Immigration Reform Law, will address current undocumented workers, DREAMers, and future migrant workers, and will establish economically sound and humane means to address once and for all our centuries-long immigration debate. The five main components of the proposal are (1) a guest worker program for future immigrant influxes that includes provisions for workers' rights and for federal aid to states; (2) passage of federal DREAM Act legislation; (3) a set of clear and stringent requirements by which undocumented immigrants currently residing in the United States can initiate a process toward citizenship; (4) a plan to encourage the best and the brightest to study in needed fields by streamlining the skilled worker visa process and granting lawful permanent resident status to immigrants who have received a master's or PhD degree from an American university in the STEM fields (science, technology, engineering, and math); and (5) effective and humane border security technologies.

Guest Workers: The Carmen Hernández–Derrick Bell Law

For practical, political, and economic reasons, a form of legalization through a guest worker program for future groups of immigrants is the most realistic option, certainly more beneficial than closing our borders (though not as beneficial as the more politically challenging option of legalization or amnesty). This portion of the larger reform bill, which I have named the Carmen Hernández–Derrick Bell Law, would resolve two issues in the immigration reform debate that have gone unaddressed: the domestic business free rider problem and the costs borne by state and local governments as a result of increases in undocumented immigration. The business community would be required to create healthcare plans for its workers and ensure workers some basic economic rights concerning wages and safety. In addition, the federal government would be required to reimburse states for their added costs associated with education and

healthcare for guest workers. Thus the proposal stipulates humane treatment to heretofore invisible, subjugated, and oppressed groups; it also provides a sound public policy solution to some of the more troubling aspects
of the current immigration divide.

College Education: The 2013 DREAM Walker–DREAM Act

The second major component of this proposal is the passage of what I
call the 2013 DREAM Walker–DREAM Act. In order to be eligible for
this expedited path toward legalization and equal treatment in terms of
the costs of college education, an undocumented college student must
have entered this country as a minor, must be enrolled and in good
standing in a four-year accredited public college or university, and must
not have a record of violence or other listed offenses to be determined
during the legislative deliberation process.

In economic terms, it makes no sense for this country to keep its best
and brightest from the opportunity to attend college without financial
discrimination. The U.S.-raised individuals subject to the DREAM Act
are effectively American in every sense of the word; they were typically
raised in this country, know only this country, and have effectively demonstrated that they are productive members of this society by their will-
ingness and preparedness to excel in higher education.

It is simply unsound and inhumane to keep a permanent underclass
because of the alleged wrongs of their parents. How could these young
people be illegal if it is a basic principle of criminal law that one is guilty of
a crime based on notions of *mens rea,* or in other words, having a criminal
intent? These young Americans have no criminal mind; indeed, they have
educational minds. DREAMers are not illegal; they are our youth.

Requirements for the Legalization Process: The Kennedy-McCain Law

The third component of this proposal for reform, which I have named
the Kennedy-McCain Law, is a plan to address the eleven million
undocumented immigrants who are currently in this country. The only

feasible and responsible way to address them is to create a path toward legalization that involves a streamlined process but also fairly stringent eligibility requirements. This streamlined option toward citizenship is not radical or even new; it is essentially the option proposed by U.S. Senators John McCain and Ted Kennedy in 2007, which ultimately was never voted on.[45] For eligibility to transition from undocumented to provisional-resident status, an individual will have to do the following:

1. pay a $5,000 fine as recognition of the individual's prior misdemeanor violation of immigration laws;
2. enroll in an approved state college or university civics and law program for at least six months; and
3. maintain a noncriminal record, with no felonies or violent acts to be determined, from the time of entering the country.

An individual who has successfully met these requirements will be placed at the "back of the line" of all other immigrants filing for legal residency status. Under no circumstance should these individuals, other than DREAMers, become citizens in less than five years.

The Bella Román STEM Visa/Residency Program

The fourth component of this five-part comprehensive plan is a program that will attract and keep the most talented students in the fields most needed in this economy. In other words, a component of this comprehensive immigration proposal must attract the "best and brightest" foreign workers and students. This part of the reform will authorize the granting of lawful permanent resident status to those who have earned a master's or PhD degree from an American university in the STEM fields (science, technology, engineering, and math). This proposal should also include a means to expedite the visa process for foreign entrepreneurs, investors, and immigrants who work in federal science and technology laboratories, provided the program has an effective means to track beneficiaries of both STEM and entrepreneur visa holders under this program.

The Enhanced Security/Humanitarian Border Protection Program

No reform will ever be deemed politically viable without appealing to the political "hawks" and those who will always believe that the southern border is unsafe (although no such anxiety has been expressed about our northern border or commercial passenger or parcel air-traffic security). Thus, any reform bill that ultimately passes will have to provide for effective and humane security technologies, such as unmanned planes and increased video monitoring, that will not only secure our borders but will also ensure that no one dies in their efforts to cross a desert or other similar naturally occurring obstacles. An additional necessary step must include a verifiable and traceable means to track visitor visas. Closing this loophole in our immigration system will be an effective means of curbing unauthorized immigrants and potential threats to the country's security.

* * *

As this book goes to press, the prospects of comprehensive immigration reform are in the headlines virtually every day in the national media. Indeed, on January 28, 2013, a bipartisan group of senators introduced their proposal for comprehensive reform. The group, known as the "Gang of Eight," consists of four Republicans and four Democrats: John McCain, Marco Rubio, Lindsey Graham, Jeff Flake, Chuck Schumer, Dick Durbin, Robert Menendez, and Michael Bennet.

> The Gang of Eight's proposal highlights 4 legislative "pillars" that must be integral to the new system. First, the plan will include a Path to Citizenship for unauthorized immigrants, contingent on the securing of the borders and implementation of a tracking system to ensure that legally admitted nonimmigrants depart when required. Second, the plan will reform the legal immigration system to emphasize the importance of individual's attributes and accomplishments that will help build the economy and "strengthen American families." Third, the plan will create an

employment verification system to prevent identity theft and end the hiring of unauthorized workers. Finally, the plan will establish an improved process for the admission of foreign workers to service our country's needs, while protecting all workers.[46]

Shortly after the announcement of the Gang of Eight's proposal, President Obama in a speech in Las Vegas endorses the efforts by the Gang of Eight, noting that it is "important for us to recognize that the foundation for bipartisan action is already in place. And if Congress is unable to move forward in a timely fashion, I will send up a bill based on my proposal and insist that they vote on it right away."[47] It thus appears that as a result of the 2012 presidential election or some other unknown basis for enlightenment, we are now in a place where comprehensive immigration reform is a real possibility.

The undocumented immigration debate has been going on in this country for well over a century. I hope that this project will help lead the way to informed debates and perhaps even eventual reform based on data rather than rhetoric. The country must end the scapegoating and stereotyping of valuable members of our society. The federal government must help state and local governments address their added education and healthcare costs associated with immigration. Finally, domestic business sectors must no longer be the missing party in the room. They cannot create the demand for undocumented immigration and reap the benefits of it without paying for it. These free riders must provide health insurance for employees, or at least employer-operated medical centers; they also need to pay additional taxes to state and local governments in regions that currently hire large numbers of undocumented immigrants. If these reforms are carried out, perhaps the value of our immigrant brothers and sisters will be recognized. They are currently invisible only because we refuse to see them.

Perhaps now is the time for a different sort of invasion—an invasion of education and activism. Young DREAMer activists, community organizers, law professors, and economists familiar with these issues, media personalities, and responsible politicians must, as called for by the Martin Luther King Center for Nonviolent Social Change, aggressively take the first step in a social movement by engaging in education efforts and making a personal commitment to see that change occur. Moreover, the domestic Latino and Latina community must not stand by quietly and merely wait for change. As Martin Luther King Jr. reminded us, "Change does not roll in on the wheels of inevitability, but comes through continuous struggle." I trust, and indeed pray, that this book, or other works like it, be the impetus to begin to change the way we see our immigrant brothers and sisters. Indeed, may we follow the prophetic words of Dr. King when he wrote from the Birmingham Jail: "We are caught in an inescapable network of mutuality, tied in a single garment of destiny. Whatever affects one directly affects all indirectly. Never again can we afford to live with the narrow, provincial 'outside agitator' idea. Anyone who lives inside the United States can never be considered an outsider."

Let us join together and see that once and for all the silent members of our society come out of the shadows and receive fair and reasonable treatment by the society so many of them have supported.

NOTES

NOTES TO CHAPTER 1

1. All direct quotes are taken from Howard Koch, *The Panic Broadcast* (New York: Avon, 1970), 36, 49–50, 58, 68, 72. The infamous *War of the Worlds* episode was originally broadcast on October 30, 1938.

2. See, e.g., William H. Calhoun, "Illegal Immigration: The Invasion Continues," Capital Hill Coffee House, Oct. 25, 2006, http://capitolhillcoffeehouse.com/more.php?id=A1528010M. "This is an invasion of America, and there is no other way to see it. Mexico, like most other third-world nations, despises the West. But they know they cannot defeat it in conventional battle, but only invade under the auspices of 'reverse colonialism.' The West contains most of the world's resources, and the third-world hordes regularly invade the West to rape and ravish it of its riches. And it is not just Mexico that invades, but all of South America, Africa, Asia, China and India are coming too."

3 See, e.g., Donald L. Barlett and James B. Steele, "Who Left the Door Open?," *Time*, Sept. 20, 2004, 51–52; see also Jack Miles, "Blacks vs. Browns," in *Arguing Immigration: The Debate over the Changing Face of America*, ed. Nicolaus Mills (New York: Touchstone, 1994). Miles likens the Los Angeles riots of 1992 to the fall of Rome.

4. Brian Tumulty and Chuck Raasch, "N.Y. License Plan Tossed: No Go for Illegal Immigrants," *Detroit Free Press*, Nov. 15, 2007, A4.

5. See, e.g., Peter Brimelow, *Alien Nation: Common Sense about America's Immigration Disaster* (New York: Random House, 1995), 271–72, arguing that minority immigrants are threatening to "break down white America's sense of identity"; Samuel P. Huntington, *Who Are We? The Challenges to America's National Identity* (New York: Simon and Schuster, 2004), 11, 19–20, expressing fear that an increasingly multicultural United States could lead to balkanization; Peter H. Schuck and Rogers M. Smith, *Citizenship without Consent: Illegal Aliens in the American Polity* (New Haven: Yale University Press, 1985), 116, arguing against birthright citizenship for children of undocumented aliens; and Michael Walzer, *Spheres of Justice: A Defense of Pluralism and Equality* (New York: Basic, 1983), 32–34, suggesting that liberal societies can deviate from norms of internal membership to restrict membership from outsiders.

6. See, e.g., Justin C. Glon, Note, "'Good Fences Make Good Neighbors': National Security and Terrorism—Time to Fence In Our Southern Border," *Indiana International and Comparative Law Review* 15 (2005): 349, 352, 361–71, suggesting the need for a fence running along the U.S.-Mexico border "to deal with" the United States' "most pressing concern."

7. See Fred Elbel, "Desert Invasion—U.S.: Illegal Immigration Invasion Numbers Analysis," http://www.desertinvasion.us/data/invasionnumbers.html (last visited Sept. 5, 2008), expressing concern that government statistics of the annual number of immigrants entering the country are grossly underestimated.

8. See, e.g., Jerry Adler, "Sweet Land of Liberties," *Newsweek*, July 10, 1995, 18, arguing that multiculturalism has resulted in a divided country; and "Immigration: Not Fixed Yet," *National Review*, June 26, 1995, 21, proposing a moratorium on immigration.

9. "FBI Report Documents Hate Crimes against Latinos at Record Level," National Association of Hispanic Journalists Blog, Nov. 20, 2007, http://nahjsblog.blogspot. com/2007/11/fbi-report-documents-hate-crimes.html. "According to the report, in 2006, Hispanics comprised 62.8% of victims of crimes motivated by a bias toward the victims' ethnicity or national origin."

10. Ibid. See, e.g., "The Dark Side of Illegal Immigration," http://www.usillegalaliens. com/impactsofillegalimmigrationcrime.html, associating illegal aliens with extremely stigmatic social dilemmas, such as violent, drug-related and sexual assault crimes, and stating, "there is just too much horrific crime being committed by illegal aliens."

11. See, e.g., Julia C. Mead, "4 Are Held in an Attack on Mexican Immigrants," *New York Times*, June 15, 2006, B7; Julia C. Mead, "Hamptons Teenager Is Accused of Menacing Hispanic Students," *New York Times*, May 9, 2006; and "Texas: Conviction in Brutal Attack," *New York Times*, Nov. 17, 2006, A22.

12. See, e.g., Lou Dobbs, "Feds' Border Action Not Nearly Enough," CNN, July 5, 2005, http://www.CNN.com/2005/US/03/31/border.agents/index.html. "Illegal immigration . . . also [raises] the larger problem of protecting our country from another deadly terrorist attack."

13. See Frank H. Wu, "The Limits of Borders: A Moderate Proposal for Immigration Reform," *Stanford Law and Policy Review* 7 (1996): 35, 36. "Under the guise of attacking 'political correctness,' immigration restrictionists have appealed to a racialized vision of citizenship."

14. For instance, a poll conducted by Quinnipiac University "found that strong majorities [of those questioned] favor[ed] building a fence along the U.S.-Mexico border, creating national ID cards for all legal residents and refusing drivers' licenses and free public education to illegal aliens." David Lightman, "Where Are Democrats on Illegal Immigration?," McClatchy, Nov. 14, 2007, http://www. mcclatchydc.com/227/story/21539.html.

15. See Ediberto Román, *Citizenship and Its Exclusions: A Classical, Constitutional, and Critical Race Critique* (New York: New York University Press, 2010).

16. Ibid., 30.
17. Emma Lazarus, "New Colossus," http://quotationsbook.com/quote/44890/.
18. Thomas Aldrich, "Unguarded Gates," in *Poems of American History*, ed. Burton Stevenson (New York: Houghton Mifflin, 1950), 659.
19. See, e.g., comments section, "SF Supervisors Urge City to Defy Federal Immigration Holds," comment by Steve, Dec. 15, 2011, http://www.sfbg.com/politics/2011/12/14/sf-supervisors-urge-city-defy-federal-immigration-holds.
20. See www.usillegalaliens.com as only one example of many anti-immigrant websites that always seem to be first on the list when one researches such issues. These sites can have a strong influence on an audience with no firsthand experience with immigrants, fueling fears and building bias, turning a would-be neutral and impartial individual into a full-blown anti-immigrant nativist who for the most part uses national security as a pretext to restrict immigration, thereby allegedly defending their own nation from an invasion.
21. In part because a major goal of this book is to put the immigration debate in its proper perspective, I will use the term "illegal" immigrant only when quoting other works. The term "illegal" is offensive in that it effectively describes an individual as a permanent criminal, essentially tainting them in perpetuity. Perhaps more importantly, the label "illegal" essentially gives license to treat these individuals as less than the collective us. It has a stigmatizing effect, which will be explored in depth here, that ultimately legitimizes all sorts of outrageous conduct and hateful speech that we do not tolerate against any other group in this country. In addition, as scholars have previously observed, the logic behind the label "illegal immigrant" is circular and conclusory. See Gerald P. Lopez, "Undocumented Mexican Migration: In Search of a Just Immigration Law and Policy," *UCLA Law Review* 28 (1981): 615, 699, n. 470.
22. Leo R. Chavez, *The Latino Threat: Constructing Immigrants, Citizens, and the Nation* (Stanford: Stanford University Press, 2008), 3.
23. Scott Nance, "Immigration Reform: After White House Meeting, Latino Officials Want to See Further Action," *Democratic Daily*, April 20, 2011, http://thedemocraticdaily.com/2011/04/20/immigration-reform-after-white-house-meeting-latino-officials-want-to-see-further-action.

NOTES TO CHAPTER 2

1. See, e.g., Michelle Malkin, *Invasion: How America Still Welcomes Terrorists, Criminals, and Other Menaces to Our Shores* (Washington, DC: Regnery, 2002).
2. Ibid., 3–4.
3. See William H. Calhoun, "Illegal Immigration: The Invasion Continues," Capital Hill Coffee House, Oct. 25, 2006, http://capitolhillcoffeehouse.com/more.php?id=A1528010M. "Our once great and noble land will be just another third-world wasteland, not unlike Mexico City or New Delhi."
4. Ibid., arguing that the United States will "become an unrecognizable amalgamation of third-world crime."

5. See "Iowa—Republicans—2008 Primary Results Exit Polls," *New York Times*, Nov. 11, 2007, http://graphics8.nytimes.com/packages/pdf/politics/20071113POLL.pdf, illustrating that a majority of Iowa Republicans believe illegal immigration is the most important problem facing the United States.

6. See Heather Mac Donald, "Crime and the Illegal Alien: The Fallout from Crippled Immigration Enforcement," Center for Immigration Studies, Washington, DC, June 2004, http://www.cis.org/articles/2004/back704.html.

7. *Cloverfield* (Paramount Pictures, 2007).

8. Kevin R. Johnson, "It's the Economy, Stupid: The Hijacking of the Debate over Immigration Reform by Monsters, Ghosts, and Goblins (or the War on Drugs, War on Terror, Narcoterrorists, Etc.)," *Chapman Law Review* 13 (2010): 583.

9. Michael A. Olivas, "The Political Efficacy of *Plyler v. Doe*: The Danger and the Discourse," *U.C. Davis Law Review* 45 (2011): 1, 14–15.

10. Lisa Flores, "Constructing Rhetorical Borders: Peons, Illegal Immigrants, and Competing Narratives of Immigration," *Critical Studies in Media Communication* 20 (2003): 362.

11. Leo R. Chavez, *The Latino Threat: Constructing Immigrants, Citizens, and the Nation* (Stanford: Stanford University Press, 2008), 2.

12. Andrea Neil Sanchez, "On Immigration, Alabama State Senator Advises Politicians to 'Empty the Clip,'" *Think Progress Security*, Feb. 8, 2011, thinkprogress.org/security/2011/02/08/176488/scott-beason-immigration.

13. "Herman Cain Proposes an Electrified Fence as Immigration Reform, Says He Was Joking," *Huffington Post*, October 18, 2011.

14. Ibid.

15. Edward Wyatt, "Cain Proposes Electrified Border Fence," *New York Times* Caucus Blog, Oct. 15, 2011, http://thecaucus.blogs.nytimes.com/2011/10/15/cain-proposes-electrified-border-fence/.

16. "Herman Cain's Electrified Border Fence 'Joke': Bad Taste?," *The Week*, Oct. 17, 2011, http://theweek.com/article/index/220394/herman-cains-electrified-border-fence-joke-bad-taste.

17. See, e.g., Immigration Profs blog, Oct. 18, 2011, http://lawprofessors.typepad.com/immigration/2011/10/herman-cain-apologizes-for-comments-on-electrifying-the-border-fence.html; and "Cain Apologizes for the Border Joke," Associated Press, Oct. 17, 2011, http://www.kpho.com/story/15716076/cain-apologizes-for-comments-on-border-fence.

18. Immigration Profs blog (quoting *Huffington Post*).

19. Russell Goldman, "Bachmann Promises to 'Double' Fence along Entire Mexican Border by 2013," *The Note*, ABC News, Oct. 15, 2011, http://abcnews.go.com/blogs/politics/2011/10/bachmann-signs-pledge-to-build-double-fence-along-entire-border-by-2013/.

20. Ibid.

21. Adam C. Smith, "Mitt Romney Takes on Immigration, with Threat of Rick Perry in the Air," *Politico*, Sept. 2, 2011, http://www.politico.com/news/stories/0911/62591.html.

22. "The 'Self-Deportation' Fantasy," editorial, *Washington Post*, Jan. 29, 2012.

23. As alluded to above, conservatives are not alone in their fear of the Mexican border. See, e.g., Glenn F. Bunting, "Boxer's Bid to Put National Guard at Border Is Stymied," *Los Angeles Times*, Aug. 6, 1994, A1.

24. Massimo Calabresi, "Is Racism Fueling the Immigration Debate?," *Time*, May 17, 2006 .

25. Ibid.

26. Mark Silva, "Drivers Licenses for Undocumented: Clinton Stumbles," *Swamp*, Oct. 31, 2007, http://www.swamppolitics.com/news/politics/blog/2007/10/driverlicensesforundocument.html.

27. See Julia Preston, "Immigration Is Defying Easy Answers," *New York Times*, Dec. 30, 2007, 17.

28. See Michelle Mittlestadt, "Dems Straddle Border; GOP Field Hawkish on Immigration," Chron.com, Nov. 11, 2007, http://www.chron.com/news/nation-world/article/Dems-straddle-border-GOP-field-hawkish-on-1650350.php.

29. "GOP Debate's Focus on Immigration Drives Coverage," *U.S. News Political Bulletin*, Nov. 30, 2007, http://www.usnews.com/usnews/politics/bulletin/bulletin071130.htm.

30. Ibid.

31. Ibid.

32. Michael Luo, "A Closer Look at the 'Sanctuary City' Argument," *New York Times*, Nov. 29, 2007.

33. Interview with John McCain, *Meet the Press,* broadcast Jan. 6, 2008, transcript available at http://www.msnbc.msn.com/id/22487036/ns/meetthepress/t/meet-press-transcript.

34. David Olinger, "Border Wars Personal Out West," *Denver Post*, Jan. 27, 2008, A16 (noting a difference for some between "the good Mexicans" and "the Latinos").

35. Ibid.

36. Ibid.

37. Tom Tancredo, interview by John Hawkins, *Right Wing News*, Feb. 26, 2012, http://www.rightwingnews.com/interviews/tancredo.php.

38. 149 Cong. Rec. H1508–09 (daily ed. Mar. 4, 2003) (statement of Sen. Tom Tancredo), http://www.gpo.gov/fdsys/pkg/CREC-2003-03-04/html/CREC-2003-03-04-pt1-PgH1507.htm.

39. "Tancredo Seeks to Make Immigration a Major Issue in Presidential Race," U.S. Border Control, June 12, 2005, available at http://classic-web.archive.org/web/20070617190933/http://www.usbc.org/info/2005/jun/tancredo.htm.

40. "Tancredo's New Ad Bomb," ABC News, Nov. 12, 2007, http://abcnews.go.com/Video/playerIndex?id=3855133; see also http://abcnews.

go.com/blogs/politics/2007/11/tancredos-explo/; and "Democrats Plot
Electoral Strategy on Immigration," Progressive States Network, Nov.
18, 2007, http://www.progressivestates.org/press/psn-in-the-news/
democrats-plot-electoral-strategy-on-immigration.

41. "Katt Williams' Anti-Mexican Rant in Phoenix: Takes on Mexican Heckler," *Huffington Post*, Aug. 29, 2011.

42. CNN Wire Staff, "Katt Williams Explains Apology for Mexico Remarks," CNN Entertainment, Sept. 3, 2011, http://
articles.cnn.com/2011-09-03/entertainment/katt.williams.
rant1apology-anti-gay-remarks-comedian-katt-williams?s=PM:SHOWBIZ.

43. Bill Carter, "CBS Drops Imus Show over Racial Remark," *New York Times*, Apr. 12, 2007.

44. Ibid.

45. Nadra Kareem Nittle, "Celebrities Who've Sparked Controversy by Using the 'N' Word," About.com, Race Relations, http://racerelations.about.com/od/hollywood/tp/Celebrities-Who-Ve-Sparked-Controversy-By-Saying-The-N-Word.htm.

46. Jolie O'Dell, "Gilbert Gottfried Fired over Japan Jokes on Twitter," Mashable.com, March 15, 2011, http://mashable.com/2011/03/15/gilbert-gottfried-japan-twitter/.

47. "Gottfried Fired as AFLAC Duck after Japanese Tsunami Tweets," *Huffington Post*, May 25, 2011.

48. See Fairness and Accuracy in Reporting, "Action Alert: GE, Microsoft Bring Bigotry to Life," Feb. 12, 2003, http://www.fair.org/index.php? page=. See also Media Matters for America, "CNN Hire Beck: Illegal Immigrants Are Either 'Terrorists,' Outlaws, or People Who 'Can't Make a Living in Their Own Dirtbag Country,'" Apr. 28, 2006, http://mediamatters.org/video/2006/04/28/cnn-hire-beck-illegal-immigrants-are-either-ter/135528.

49. Leadership Conference on Civil Rights Education Fund, "Confronting the New Faces of Hate: Hate Crimes in America, 2009," http://www.civilrights.org/publications/hatecrimes/escalating-violence.html.

50. Calabresi, "Is Racism Fueling the Immigration Debate?"

51. Shortly after making his mathematically challenged comments concerning the demographic shift in this country, Gibson responded to criticism of his "make more babies" comment in a subsequent "My Word" segment. He stated that there were "some misunderstandings" regarding his earlier comments, and that "my concern was simply that I didn't want America to become Europe, where the birth rate is so low the continent is fast being populated by immigrants, mainly from Muslim countries." Ben Armbruster, "Gibson Responded to Criticism of 'Make More Babies' Remarks—By Invoking Europe's Rising Muslim Population," Media Matters for America, May 18, 2006, http://mediamatters.org/video/2006/05/18/gibson-responded-to-criticism-of-make-more-babi/135726.

52. Andrew Ironside, "O'Reilly: Supporters of Liberalizing Immigration Bill Want to 'Change the Complexion' of America," Media Matters, May 31, 2007,

http://mediamatters.org/video/2007/05/31/oreilly-supporters-of-liberalizing-immigration/138980. See also Andrew Dobbs, "Bill O'Reilly Is a Racist," Burnt Orange Report, March 30, 2004, http://www.burntorangereport.com/mt/archives/2004/03/bill_oreilly_is.html.

53. Andrew Walzer, "Boortz: 'I Don't Care If Mexicans Pile Up,'" Media Matters, June 18, 2007, http://mediamatters.org/mobile/video/2007/06/18/boortz-i-dont-care-if-mexicans-pile-up-against/139114. Also see Justin Raimondo, "Boot Boortz!," Antiwar.com, Nov. 26, 2003, http://www.antiwar.com/justin/jspecial112603.html.

54. Michael Maio, "Savage Called Latino Advocacy Group 'the Ku Klux Klan of the Hispanic People,'" Media Matters, May 18, 2007, http://mediamatters.org/research/2007/05/18/savage-called-latino-advocacy-group-the-ku-klux/138899.

55. See "Who Is on UK 'Least Wanted' List," BBC News, May 5, 2009, http://news.bbc.co.uk/2/hi/uk_news/8033319.stm; Raphael G. Satter, "Michael Savage Banned from Entering UK," Huffington Post, May 5, 2009; and "U.S. 'Hate List' DJ to Sue Britain," BBC News, May 6, 2009, http://news.bbc.co.uk/2/hi/8035114.stm.

56. Kathleen Henehan, "Savage on Immigrant Students' Hunger Strike," Media Matters, July 6, 2007, http://mediamatters.org/video/2007/07/06/savage-on-immigrant-students-hunger-strike-let/139270.

57. Anti-Defamation League, "Patrick Buchanan: Over the Line," http://www.adl.org/special_reports/Patrick_Buchanan2/Buchanan%20report.pdf. For an array of quotes, articles, and other information about Buchanan, see ADL, "Pat Buchanan in His Own Words," http://www.adl.org/special_reports/buchanan_own_words/buchanan_intro.asp. On paleoconservatism, see Joseph Scotchie, ed., *The Paleo-conservatives: New Voices of the Old Right* (New Brunswick, NJ: Transaction, 1999); Paul Gottfried, *The Conservative Movement* (New York: Twayne, 1993); and the "What Is Paleoconservatism?" symposium in *Chronicles* magazine, January 2001. See also Buchanan's books *State of Emergency: The Third World Invasion and Conquest of America* (New York: St. Martin's Griffin, 2006); and *The Death of the West: How Dying Populations and Immigrant Invasions Imperil Our Country and Civilization* (New York: St. Martin's Griffin, 2002).

58. See "Lou Dobbs Tonight: Examination of Issues Arising from Illegal Aliens in the U.S.," CNN broadcast, March 21, 2005, transcript available at http://transcripts.cnn.com/TRANSCRIPTS/0503/21/ldt.01.html. Dobbs's alien invasion references continued even to the program's end, where he concluded the evening's episode by saying, "Please join us tomorrow—the invasion of illegal aliens into this country, our special reports continue. We'll be reporting on the government's failure to enforce our immigration laws, and how that led to a state of emergency in one county."

59. Leadership Conference, "Confronting the New Faces of Hate."

60. Heidi Beirich, "Getting Immigration Facts Straight," Southern Poverty Law Center, *Intelligence Report*, summer 2007, http://www.splcenter.org/get-informed/intelligence-report/browse-all-issues/2007/summer/paranoid-style-redux/getting-immigrat.

61. Quoted in Leadership Conference, "Confronting the New Faces of Hate." See also "AILA Supports the Launch of NCLR's 'We Can Stop the Hate' Campaign," AILA InfoNet, Doc. No. 08020132, Feb. 1, 2008.

62. See Fred Hiatt, "How to Save Immigration Reform," *Washington Post*, June 26, 2006, A21; see also John W. Mashek, "How Talk Radio Torpedoed Immigration Reform," A Capital View blog, July 3, 2007, http:// www.usnews.com/blogs/ mashek/2007/7/3/how-talk-radio-torpedoed-immigration-reform.html.

63. "Pelosi: 'Hate Radio' Hijacked Political Discourse with 'Xenophobic, Anti-Immigrant' Rhetoric," Think Progress, June 28, 2007, http://thinkprogress.org/ politics/2007/06/28/14368/pelosi-talk-radio/. For additional examples of talk radio's attacks, see Media Matters, "Savage's Trifecta: Smears of Hispanics, Gays, and Jews," May 12, 2006, http://majorityrights.com/P2585/P1625, which describes Michael Savage as saying, "'Our brown brethren' entering the United States may 'erase' the 'European-American, or the white person,' who . . . is more 'benevolent' and 'enlightened.'"; see also "Rush Limbaugh Show: Illegal Immigration," radio broadcast, uploaded May 14, 2007, http://www.youtube.com/watch?v=ZHPm_TEQ0PA.

64. Interview with John McCain, *Meet the Press*.

65. "McCain's Border Dance Continues, Says Democratic National Committee," *Hispanic Business*, http://www.hispanicbusiness.com/news/newsbyid. asp?idx=98199&page=2&cat=&more.

66. N. C. Aizenman, "Small-Town Residents Helped to Seal Defeat," *Washington Post*, June 29, 2007, A1.

67. See, e.g., Lawrence Auster, *The Path to National Suicide: An Essay on Immigration and Multiculturalism* (Monterey, VA: American Immigration Control Foundation, 1990), http://jtl.org/auster/PNS.pdf; and Richard D. Lamm and Gary Imhoff, *The Immigration Time Bomb: The Fragmenting of America* (New York: Truman Talley, 1985), 1–11, 76–87.

68. Heidi Beirich and Mark Potok, "CNN's Lou Dobbs Refuses to Cover Anti-Latino Racism in Anti-Immigration Activist Groups," Southern Poverty Law Center, *Intelligence Report*, Winter 2005, http://www.splcenter.org/get-informed/ intelligence-report/browse-all-issues/2005/winter/broken-record.

69. Ibid.

70. Campaign for a United America, "Voices of Intolerance—Jim Gilchrist Minuteman Project," accessed July 30, 2012, http://cua.newcomm.org/index. php?option=com_content&task=view&id=16&Itemid=27.

71. Heidi Beirich, "The Nativist Lobby: Three Faces of Intolerance," ed. Mark Potok, Southern Poverty Law Center, February 2009, 4, http://cdna.splcenter.org/sites/ default/files/downloads/splc_nativistlobby.pdf.

72. Ibid., 9.

73. Anti-Defamation League, "Immigrants Targeted: Extremist Rhetoric Moves into the Mainstream," 2008, http://www.adl.org/civil_rights/anti_immigrant/Immigrants%20Targeted%20UPDATE_2008.pdf.

74. Ibid.
75. Leadership Conference, "Confronting the New Faces of Hate."
76. Kimber Solana, "Molotov Cocktail Thrown at Immigrant Rights Advocate's Home," *Racine (WI) Journal Times*, June 1, 2011, http://www.journaltimes.com/news/local/articleeb4a290e-8c42-11e0-a335-001cc4c03286.html. The illegal immigrant/alien hunting bumper sticker closely resembles an authentic state hunting permit and adheres to a vehicle's rear window or bumper. Typically, they can be found at many rural gas stations, being in high demand with the local nativists. Ironically, and very likely ignorantly, those same nativists purchase their gasoline and other frequently needed products from foreign-owned and -operated entities that employ native-born locals who merely appear to own and run the establishment. It is unfortunate what many immigrants must do to stay in business due to prejudice and bias. Moreover, many of these foreign-born store owners are now naturalized U.S. citizens, so to appease certain locals, they state that the store is "American owned and operated," as they are in fact hardworking, taxpaying American citizens.
77. Steve Strunsky, "Report: Newark Airport Screeners Targeted Mexicans," *Newark Star Ledger*, June 12, 2011, http://www.nj.com/news/index.ssf/2011/06/reportnewarkairportscreener.html.
78. "Debate Still Simmers over NY Hate Crime Stabbing," Fox News, Sept. 19, 2011, http://www.foxnews.com/us/2011/09/19/debate-still-simmers-over-ny-hate-crime-stabbing-2024726399/; Robert Smith, "New York Teen Convicted in Hate Crime Death," NPR.org, April 19, 2010, http://www.npr.org/templates/story/story.php?storyId=126114983.
79. Ibid.
80. Smith, "New York Teen Convicted in Hate Crime Death."
81. Kirk Semple, "Youth Indicted in Staten Island Hate Crime Assault," *New York Times*, Sept. 29, 2011; Kirk Semple, "Attacks on Mexicans Leave Neighborhood in Turmoil," *New York Times*, July 30, 2010.
82. "3 Charged in San Francisco Hate Crime on Mexicans," CBS News, March 17, 2011, http://sanfrancisco.cbslocal.com/2011/03/17/3-charged-in-san-francisco-hate-crime-attack-on-mexicans/. Hate crime enhancements increase the penalties for crimes such as battery, assault, and harassment that involve race, ethnicity, sexual preference, or religious beliefs as a motivation or controlling element in the crime.
83. Ari Burack, "District Attorney George Gascon Says Hate Crimes on the Rise in San Francisco," *San Francisco Examiner*, March 18, 2011.
84. Elise Foley, "Shawna Forde Sentenced to Death for Double Murder in Arizona," *Huffington Post*, Sept. 29, 2011.
85. Ibid.
86. Leadership Conference, "Confronting the New Faces of Hate." See also "Men Get Prison Sentence in Mexican Immigrant Death," Reuters, Feb. 23, 2011, http://www.reuters.com/article/2011/02/24/us-crime-hate-idUSTRE71M7IY20110224.

87. Michael Rubinkam and Kathy Matheson, "Feds Suspect Cover-Up in Shenandoah Beating Death," Associated Press, Dec. 16, 2009, available at http://citizensvoice. com/news/feds-suspect-cover-up-in-shenandoah-beating-death-1.490910.

88. Sabrina Tavernise, "2 Pennsylvania Men Found Guilty in 2008 Killing of Mexican," *New York Times*, Oct. 14, 2010.

89. Max Blumenthal, "Hosting Segment from Hazleton, Pa., Dobbs Did Not Acknowledge Fundraising for the Embattled Town," Media Matters, May 9, 2007, http://mediamatters.org/research/2007/05/09/ hosting-segment-from-hazleton-pa-dobbs-did-not/138822.

90. Ibid.

91. Leadership Conference, "Confronting the New Faces of Hate." See also Sean D. Hamill, "Mexican's Death Bares a Town's Ethnic Tension," *New York Times*, Aug. 5, 2008.

92. "Hate Crimes against Immigrants and Hispanics Increase," Trans-Border News Blog, July 11, 2011, http://transborder.wordpress.com/2011/07/11/ hate-crimes-against-immigrants-and-hispanics-increase/.

93. Leadership Conference, "Confronting the New Faces of Hate."

94. Ibid.

95. See, e.g., Ben Armbruster, "Gibson: 'Make More Babies,'" Media Matters, May 12, 2006, http://mediamatters.org/research/2006/05/12/ gibson-make-more-babies-because-in-twenty-five/135674.

96. The anti-immigration advocates have also attempted to invoke a legal basis for their characterization of the so-called invasion. Some have pointed to the "Invasion Clause" of the U.S. Constitution, which provides that the "United States shall protect every state against invasion," to justify the need for a fence running across the U.S.-Mexico border. Justin C. Glon, Note, "'Good Fences Make Good Neighbors': National Security and Terrorism—Time to Fence In Our Southern Border," *Indiana International and Comparative Law Review* 15 (2005): 375. This use of legal doctrine to characterize immigration as an invasion fails to consider that, in terms of the effect on the population, immigration simply does not approach the level of invasion. Additionally, the use of the invasion clause is legally questionable and more likely merely another irresponsible means to promote fear and hatred of the foreigner.

97. Andres Oppenheimer, "Time to Hit Back against Anti-Latino Bigotry," *Miami Herald*, July 22, 2007, A14.

98. See Lani Guinier and Gerald Torres, *The Miner's Canary: Enlisting Race, Resisting Power, Transforming Democracy* (Cambridge: Harvard University Press, 2002), 237–53.

99. See, e.g., Heidi Beirich and Mark Potok, "Keeping America White," Southern Poverty Law Center, *Intelligence Report*, Winter 2003, 31, http://www.splcenter. org/intel/intelreport/article.jsp?aid=152.

100. Calabresi, "Is Racism Fueling the Immigration Debate?"

101. Ibid.
102. Ressam was captured near the Washington-Canada border en route to detonate explosives at Los Angeles International Airport on the last New Year's Eve of the millennium. United States v. Ressam, 474 F.3d 597, 600 (9th Cir. 2007), rev'd on other grounds, 128 S. Ct. 1858 (2008); see also National Commission on Terrorist Attacks, *The 9/11 Commission Report* (New York: Norton, 2004), 236–37.

NOTES TO CHAPTER 3

1. Mark Silva, "Drivers Licenses for Undocumented: Clinton Stumbles," *The Swamp*, Oct. 31, 2007, http://www.swamppolitics.com/news/politics/blog/2007/10/driverlicensesforundocument.html.
2. Leo R. Chavez, *The Latino Threat: Constructing Immigrants, Citizens, and the Nation* (Stanford: Stanford University Press, 2008), 26–36.
3. Heidi Beirich, "Getting Immigration Facts Straight," Southern Poverty Law Center, *Intelligence Report*, Summer 2007, http://www.splcenter.org/get-informed/intelligence-report/browse-all-issues/2007/summer/paranoid-style-redux/getting-immigrat.
4. Central Intelligence Agency, "Mexico," in *The World Fact Book*, https://www.cia.gov/library/publications/the-world-factbook/geos/mx.html.
5. Beirich, "Getting Immigration Facts Straight."
6. Ibid.
7. Julian L. Simon, *Immigration: The Demographic and Economic Facts* (Washington, DC: Cato Institute and National Immigration Forum, 1995).
8. National Research Council, *The Immigration Debate: Studies on the Economic, Demographic, and Fiscal Effects of Immigration*, ed. James P. Smith and Barry Edmonston, Panel on the Demographic and Economic Impacts of Immigration (Washington, DC: National Academies Press, 1998), 10.
9. Susan B. Carter and Richard Sutch, "Historical Background to Current Immigration Issues," in National Research Council, *The Immigration Debate*, 290.
10. Ibid., 297.
11. Ibid., 298, fig. 8-6.
12. Daniel Griswold, "Comprehensive Immigration Reform: Finally Getting It Right," Center for Free Trade Policy Studies, May 16, 2007, http://www.cato.org/pubs/ftb/FTB-029.pdf.
13. Julia Preston, "Immigration at Record Level, Analysis Finds," *New York Times*, Nov. 29, 2007.
14. Jeffrey S. Passel and D'Vera Cohn, "U.S. Unauthorized Immigration Flows Are Down Sharply Since Mid-Decade," Pew Hispanic Center, Sept. 1, 2010, http://pewhispanic.org/reports/report.php?ReportID=126.
15. Beirich, "Getting Immigration Facts Straight."
16. Jack Martin, "Illegal Aliens and Crime Incidence," FAIR, http://www.fairus.org/site/DocServer/crimestudy.pdf?docID=2321, quoted in "Does Illegal Immigration

Relate to Higher Crime Incidence?," ProCon.org, Jan. 8, 2008, http://immigration. procon.org/view.answers.php?questionID=000782.

17. Deborah Schurman-Kauflin, "The Dark Side of Illegal Immigration," quoted in "Does Illegal Immigration Relate to Higher Crime Incidence?"

18. Family Security Matters, "Illegal Aliens Kill More Americans Than Iraq War," http://www.freerepublic.com/focus/f-news/1834117/posts, quoted in "Does Illegal Immigration Relate to Higher Crime Incidence?"

19. John Hagan and Alberto Palloni, "Immigration and Crime in the United States," in National Research Council, *The Immigration Debate*, 369–70.

20. Ibid., 381.

21. Ibid.

22. Kristen F. Butcher and Anne Morrison Piehl, "Why Are Immigrants' Incarceration Rates So Low? Evidence on Selective Immigration, Deterrence and Deportation," Federal Reserve Bank of Chicago, Working Paper no. 2005-19, 2005.

23. Beirich, "Getting Immigration Facts Straight."

24. Emily Deruy, "Children of Immigrants More Educated Than Their Peers," ABC News/Univision, Feb. 14, 2013, http://abcnews.go.com/ABC_Univision/Politics/ success-generation-immigrants/story?id=18501089.

25. William F. McDonald, July 12, 2006 testimony before the U.S. Senate Committee on the Judiciary hearing entitled "Examining the Need for Comprehensive Immigration Reform, Part II." Quoted in "Does Illegal Immigration Relate to Higher Crime Incidence?"

26. Rubén G. Rumbaut and Walter A. Ewing, "The Myth of Immigrant Criminality and the Paradox of Assimilation: Incarceration Rates among Native and Foreign-Born Men," Immigration Policy Center, American Immigration Law Foundation, Spring 2007, http://www.immigrationpolicy.org/sites/default/files/docs/Imm%20 Criminality%20(IPC).pdf, quoted in "Does Illegal Immigration Relate to Higher Crime Incidence?"

27. Kristin A. Butcher and Anne Morrison Piehl, "Crime, Corrections, and California," *California Counts*, vol. 9, February 2008, http://www.ppic.org/content/pubs/ cacounts/CC_208KBCC.pdf.

28. Christopher Dickey, "Reading, Ranting, and Arithmetic," *Daily Beast*, May 26, 2010, http://www.thedailybeast.com/newsweek/2010/05/27/reading-ranting-and-arithmetic.html.

29. Demetrios G. Papademetriou, "The Global Struggle with Illegal Migration: No End in Sight," Migration Information Source, Sept. 1, 2005, http://www.migrationinformation.org/feature/display.cfm?id=336.

30. See, e.g., Larry J. Obhof, Comment, "The Irrationality of Enforcement? An Economic Analysis of U.S. Immigration Law," *Kansas Journal of Law and Public Policy* 12 (2002): 163, 174–76.

31. Kevin R. Johnson, *Opening the Floodgates: Why America Needs to Rethink Its Borders and Immigration Laws* (New York: New York University Press, 2007), 132.

32. Walter A. Ewing, "From Denial to Acceptance: Effectively Regulating Immigration to the United States," *Stanford Law and Policy Review* 16 (2005): 445–46.

33. See Chris Nuttall, "Intel Chief Calls for Easing of Visa Curbs," *Financial Times*, Feb. 8, 2006, 6.

34. American Farm Bureau Federation, "Impact of Migrant Labor Restrictions on the Agricultural Sector," February 2006, 1, http://www.immigrationworks-usa.org/uploaded/file/AFB_Labor_Study_February2006.pdf. See also Huyen Pham and Pham Hoang Van, "The Economic Impact of Local Immigration Regulation: An Empirical Analysis," *Cardozo Law Review* 32, no. 2 (November 2010).

35. John Kenneth Galbraith, *The Nature of Mass Poverty* (Cambridge: Harvard University Press, 1979), 134.

36. Robert Rector, Christine Kim, and Shanea Watkins, "The Fiscal Cost of Low-Skill Households to the U.S. Taxpayer," Heritage Foundation Special Report no. 12, April 4, 2007, http://www.heritage.org/research/reports/2007/04/the-fiscal-cost-of-low-skill-households-to-the-us-taxpayer.

37. Daniel Griswold, "The Fiscal Impact of Immigration Reform: The Real Story," Cato Institute, Free Trade Bulletin no. 30, May 21, 2007, http://www.cato.org/publications/free-trade-bulletin/fiscal-impact-immigration-reform-real-story.

38. "Heritage Foundation Promotes Study Even the GOP Hates," Crooks and Liars, May 19, 2013, http://crooksandliars.com/karoli/heritage-foundation-promotes-immigration-st/.

39. "Juan Williams Breaks Down the Controversial Heritage Foundation Study on Immigration," Fox News Latino, May 10, 2013, http://latino.foxnews.com/latino/opinion/2013/05/10/juan-williams-breaks-down-controversial-heritage-foundation-study-on/. Interestingly, shortly after the appearance of this story, Richwine resigned from the Heritage Foundation.

40. Ronald D. Lee and Timothy W. Miller, "The Current Fiscal Impact of Immigrants and Their Descendants: Beyond the Immigrant Household," in National Research Council, *The Immigration Debate*, 194.

41. Ibid., 200.

42. "Immigration Policy: An Overview," Hearing before the Subcommittee on Immigration of the Senate Committee on the Judiciary, 107th Cong. (2001) (statement of Stephen Moore, Senior Fellow in Economics, Cato Institute), 19, http://www.loc.gov/law/find/hearings/pdf/00092836952.pdf.

43. Ibid.

44. Ibid., 20.

45. Ibid., 20–21.

46. Ibid., 21.

47. Ibid., 22.

48. Peter B. Dixon, Maureen T. Rimmer, and Martin Johnson, "Reducing Illegal Migrants in the U.S.: A Dynamic CGE Analysis," Centre of Policy Studies and the

Impact Project, General Paper No. G-183, July 2008, 28, http://www.monash.edu.
au/policy/ftp/workpapr/g-183.pdf.

49. Ibid., 32.
50. Ibid., 35.
51. Ibid., 5.
52. Ibid., 61.
53. Peter B. Dixon and Maureen T. Rimmer, "Restriction or Legalization? Measuring
the Economic Benefits of Immigration Reform," Cato Institute, Center for Trade
Policy Studies, no. 40, Aug. 13, 2009, 1, http://www.cato.org/pubs/tpa/tpa-040.pdf.
54. Ibid., 2.
55. Ibid., 3.
56. Ibid., 4.
57. Ibid., 13.
58. Gordon H. Hanson, "The Economics and Policy of Illegal Immigration in the
United States," Migration Policy Institute, 2009, 4, http://www.migrationpolicy.
org/pubs/Hanson-Dec09.pdf.
59. Ibid., 5.
60. Raúl Hinojosa-Ojeda, "Raising the Floor for American Workers: The Economic
Benefits of Comprehensive Immigration Reform," Immigration Policy Center,
Center for American Progress, January 2010, 1, http://www.americanprogress.org/
wp-content/uploads/2012/09/immigrationeconreport3.pdf.
61. Ibid.
62. Ibid., 1–2.
63. Ibid., 2.
64. Ibid., 11–12.
65. Ibid., 2.
66. Ibid., 12.
67. Ibid., 5–6.
68. Ibid., 3.
69. Peter B. Dixon, Martin Johnson, and Maureen T. Rimmer, "Economy-Wide
Effects of Reducing Illegal Immigrants in U.S. Employment," *Contemporary Economic Policy* 29, no. 1 (2011): 14.
70. Ibid., 18, 22.
71. Ibid., 29.
72. Beirich, "Getting Immigration Facts Straight."
73. George J. Borjas, Jeffrey Grogger, and Gordon H. Hanson, "Imperfect Substitution
between Immigrants and Natives: A Reappraisal," National Bureau of Economic
Research, Working Paper 13887, March 2008, 30, http://www.nber.org/papers/w13887.
74. Gianmarco I. P. Ottaviano and Giovanni Peri, "Rethinking the Gains from Immigration: Theory and Evidence from the U.S.," National Bureau of Economic Research,
Working Paper 11672, September 2005, 27, http://www.nber.org/papers/w11672.

75. Gianmarco I. P. Ottaviano and Giovanni Peri, "Rethinking the Effects of Immigration on Wages," National Bureau of Economic Research, Working Paper 12497, August 2006, 34, http://www.nber.org/papers/w12497.

76. Council of Economic Advisers, "Immigration's Economic Impact," June 20, 2007, http://georgewbush-whitehouse.archives.gov/cea/cea_immigration_062007.html.

77. Giovanni Peri and Chad Sparber, "Task Specialization, Immigration, and Wages," *American Economic Journal: Applied Economics* 1, no. 3 (July 2009): 135-69 (can also be found as Centre for Research and Analysis of Migration, Discussion Paper, CDP No 02/08, January 2009, 2, http://www.cream-migration.org/publ_uploads/CDP_02_08.pdf).

78. Ibid., 1.

79. Ibid., 2.

80. David Card, "Immigration and Inequality," Centre for Research and Analysis of Migration, Discussion Paper Series, 2009, i, http://www.cream-migration.org/publ_uploads/CDP_07_09.pdf.

81. Ibid., 3.

82. Robert J. Shapiro and Jiwon Vellucci, "The Impact of Immigration and Immigration Reform on the Wages of American Workers," New Policy Institute, May 2010, 1, http://www.immigrationworksusa.org/uploaded/file/NPI_Report_Shapiro_5_26_10.pdf.

83. Ibid.

84. Ibid., 10.

85. Ibid.

86. Ibid., 3.

87. Beirich, "Getting Immigration Facts Straight."

88. Rakesh Kochhar, "Growth in the Foreign-Born Workforce and Employment of the Native Born," Pew Hispanic Center, Aug. 10, 2006, 27, http://www.pewhispanic.org/2006/08/10/growth-in-the-foreign-born-workforce-and-employment-of-the-native-born/.

89. Rob Paral and Associates, "Untying the Knot: Immigration and Native-Born Unemployment across Racial/Ethnic Groups," Immigration Policy Center Special Report, May 2009, 2–3, http://www.immigrationpolicy.org/special-reports/untying-knot-series-unemployment-and-immigration.

90. Giovanni Peri, "The Effect of Immigrants on U.S. Employment and Productivity," FRBSF Economic Letter, Aug. 30, 2010, 1, http://www.frbsf.org/publications/economics/letter/2010/el2010-26.pdf.

91. Ibid.

92. Emily A. Harrell and David L. Franklin, "The Economic Realities of Immigration in the United States: Implications for Policy," 2008, unpublished manuscript, http:// works.bepress.com/cgi/viewcontent.cgi?article=1002&context=emily_harrell.

93. See Michael A. Olivas, "Preempting Preemption: Foreign Affairs, State Rights, and Alienage Classifications," *Virginia Journal of International Law* 35 (1994): 217, 223–25 (on the question of whether immigration policy should be "regulated by the individual states rather than being preempted by federal powers").

94. Thank you to Professors Andre Smith and Victor Romero for encouraging me to confront the question of whether all anti-immigrant stances are race-based and therefore bigoted. Blaming all criticism of immigration on racism can not only miss valuable insights, it can create a divide that can serve to stifle, instead of promote, honest engagement.

NOTES TO CHAPTER 4

1. See, e.g., Michael A. Olivas, "Preempting Preemption: Foreign Affairs, State Rights, and Alienage Classifications," *Virginia Journal of International Law* 35 (1994): 227–28.

2. U.S. General Accounting Office, "Illegal Alien Schoolchildren: Issues in Estimating State-by-State Costs," Report to the Chairman, Committee on the Judiciary, House of Representatives, GAO-04-733, June 2004, 3–4.

3. See Personal Responsibility and Work Opportunity Reconciliation Act of 1996, Pub. L. No. 104-193, 110 Stat. 2105 (1996).

4. See Julia Field Costich, "Legislating a Public Health Nightmare: The Anti-Immigrant Provisions of the 'Contract with America' Congress," *Kentucky Law Journal* 90 (2002): 1043, 1063.

5. See Illegal Immigration Reform and Immigrant Responsibility Act of 1996, Pub. L. No. 104-208, 110 Stat. 3009 (1996) (enacted as Division C of the Omnibus Consolidated Appropriations Act, 1997).

6. Robert J. Shapiro and Jiwon Vellucci, "The Impact of Immigration and Immigration Reform on the Wages of American Workers," New Policy Institute, May 2010, http://www.immigrationworksusa.org/uploaded/file/NPI_Report_Shapiro_5_26_10.pdf.

7. Ibid., 17.

8. GAO, "Illegal Alien Schoolchildren," 28.

9. U.S. General Accounting Office, "Undocumented Aliens: Questions Persist about Their Impact on Hospitals' Uncompensated Care Costs," Report to Congressional Requesters, May 2004, 21.

10. James J. Kielkopf, "The Economic Impact of Undocumented Workers in Minnesota," Hispanic Advocacy and Community Empowerment through Research, September 2000, 15, http://www.hacer-mn.org/downloads/english_reports/EconomicImpactUndocumentedWorkers.pdf.

11. New Mexico Fiscal Policy Project, "Undocumented Immigrants in New Mexico: State Tax Contributions and Fiscal Concerns," May 2006.

12. Oregon Center for Public Policy, "Undocumented Workers Are Taxpayers Too," April 2006, 4, http://www.ocpp.org/2007/issue070410immigranttaxeseng.pdf.

13. Beth Pearson and Michael F. Sheehan, "Undocumented Immigrants in Iowa: Estimated Tax Contributions and Fiscal Impact," Iowa Policy Project, Oct. 2007, http://www.iowapolicyproject.org/2007docs/071025-undoc.pdf.

14. "Breaking the Piggy Bank: How Illegal Immigration Is Sending Schools into the Red," Federation for American Immigration Reform, http://www.fairus.org/publications/breaking-the-piggy-bank-how-illegal-immigration-is-sending-schools-into-the-red-updated-2005?A=SearchResult&SearchID=3248030&ObjectID=5123319&ObjectType=35; "The Costs of Illegal Immigration to Californians," Federation for American Immigration Reform, 2004, http://usgovinfo.about.com/od/immigrationnaturalizatio/a/caillegals.htm.

15. Philip J. Romero, "Racing Backwards: The Fiscal Impact of Illegal Immigration in California, Revisited," *Social Contract* 17, no. 4 (Summer 2007), http://www.thesocialcontract.com/artman2/publish/tsc_17_4/tsc_17_4_romero_printer.shtml.

16. Americas Society, "The Economic Impact of Immigrant-Related Local Ordinances," 2011, 6, http://www.as-coa.org/sites/default/files/ASImmigrationWhitePaper.pdf.

17. Stephanie Sandoval, "FB Studies Tough Provisions Aimed at Illegal Immigrants," *Dallas Morning News*, Aug. 21, 2006, A1; also available at http://www.tech-zone360.com/news/2006/08/21/1818750.htm.

18. Michael J. Almonte, Note, "State and Local Law Enforcement Response to Undocumented Immigrants: Can We Make the Rules, Too?," *Brooklyn Law Review* 72 (2007): 655–66.

19. Americas Society, "The Economic Impact of Immigrant-Related Local Ordinances," 5.

20. Ibid., 18.

21. Amy Howe, "Court to Consider Arizona Immigration Law: A Preview in Plain English," Supreme Court Blog, April 25, 2012, http://www.scotusblog.com/?p=143796.

22. Immigration Policy Center, "How Much Will Arizona's Immigration Bill (SB1070) Cost?," press release, April 24, 2010, http://www.immigrationpolicy.org/newsroom/release/how-much-will-arizonas-immigration-bill-sb1070-cost.

23. "Deficits, Lawsuits, Diminished Public Safety: Your State Can't Afford SB 1070," National Immigration Forum, Dec. 30, 2010, www.immigrationforum.org/images/uploads/2010/SB1070Report.pdf.

24. Raúl Hinojosa-Ojeda and Marshall Fitz, "A Rising Tide or a Shrinking Pie: The Economic Impact of Legalization versus Deportation," Center for American Progress and Immigration Policy Center, March 24, 2011, http://www.americanprogress.org/issues/immigration/report/2011/03/24/9250/a-rising-tide-or-a-shrinking-pie/.

25. Ibid.

26. Ibid.

27. Amy Howe, "SB 1070: In Plain English," Supreme Court Blog, June 25, 2012, http://www.scotusblog.com/2012/06/s-b-1070-in-plain-english/.

28. Available at http://www1.legis.ga.gov/legis/2011_12/sum/hb87.htm.
29. Jeremy Redmon, "New Report: Georgia 7th among States for Illegal Immigrants," *Atlanta Journal Constitution*, Feb. 2, 2011.
30. Southern Poverty Law Center, "SPLC Launches Federal Court Challenge to Alabama's Discriminatory Anti-Immigrant Law," July 8, 2011, http://www.splcenter.org/get-informed/news/splc-launches-federal-court-challenge-to-alabama-s-discriminatory-anti-immigration.
31. Southern Poverty Law Center, "SPLC Vows to Challenge Racist Alabama Immigration Law," June 14, 2011, http://www.splcenter.org/get-informed/news/splc-vows-to-challenge-racist-alabama-immigration-law.
32. Samuel Addy, "A Cost-Benefit Analysis of the New Alabama Immigration Law," January 2012, http://cber.cba.ua.edu/New%20AL%20Immigration%20Law%20-%20Costs%20and%20Benefits.pdf.
33. Ibid., 9.
34. "Alabama Lawmakers Call for Immigration Law Repeal," Fox News Latino, Feb. 28, 2012, http://latino.foxnews.com/latino/politics/2012/02/28/alabama-lawmakers-calls-for-immigration-law-repeal/.
35. "Alabama's Immigration Law Results in Arrests of Foreign Business Leaders," Equal Justice Initiative, Dec. 1, 2011, http://www.eji.org/eji/node/585.
36. Campbell Robertson, "Critics See 'Chilling Effect' in Alabama Immigration Law," *New York Times*, Oct. 27, 2011.
37. "Setback for Rogue Immigration Laws," editorial, *New York Times*, Aug. 21, 2012.
38. Carl Krueger, "In-State Tuition for Undocumented Immigrants," Education Commission of the States, *State Notes*, August 2006, 1, http://www.ecs.org/clearinghouse/61/00/6100.htm#_edn1.
39. Quoted in http://www.dreamactivist.org/statement-of-senator-orrin-hatch-on-the-dream-act/.
40. Michael Olivas, *No Undocumented Child Left Behind* (New York: New York University Press, 2012), 69–71.
41. Mark Whittington, "Texas Dream Act Provides In-State Tuition to Children of Illegal Aliens," Oct. 19, 2011, http://news.yahoo.com/texas-dream-act-provides-state-tuition-children-illegal-195700309.html.
42. Leslie Berestein Rojas, "Readers Gone Wild (On the California Dream Act)," Southern California Public Radio, Oct. 9, 2011, http://multiamerican.scpr.org/2011/10/readers-gone-wild-on-the-california-dream-act/.
43. Saskia de Melker, "California 'Dream Act' Offers Undocumented Students Path to Higher Education," *PBS NewsHour*, Oct. 17, 2011, http://www.pbs.org/newshour/rundown/2011/10/california-dream.html.
44. Krueger, "In-State Tuition for Undocumented Immigrants."
45. Ediberto Román and Christopher B. Carbot, "Freeriders and Diversity in the Legal Academy: A New Dirty Dozen List?," *Indiana Law Journal* 83, no. 4 (October 2008): 1247–48.

NOTES TO CHAPTER 5

1. See John F. Kennedy, *A Nation of Immigrants* (New York: Harper and Row, 1964).
2. See Kevin R. Johnson, "The Forgotten 'Repatriation' of Persons of Mexican Ancestry and Lessons for the 'War on Terror,'" *Pace Law Review* 26 (2005): 45.
3. The use of stigma and stereotyping is obviously not limited to ethnic and racial minorities. Legal scholars have examined a variety of the effects of stigma on other outsider groups. See, e.g., William N. Eskridge Jr., "No Promo Homo: The Sedimentation of Antigay Discourse and the Channeling Effect of Judicial Review," *New York University Law Review* 75 (2000): 1327, 1331–32.
4. U.S. Const. art. I, § 8, cl. 4, § 9, cl. 1.
5. Paul Brickner and Meghan Hanson, "The American Dreamers: Racial Prejudices and Discrimination as Seen through the History of American Immigration Law," *Thomas Jefferson Law Review* 26 (2004): 203, 204.
6. Act of Mar. 26, 1790, ch. 3, 1 Stat. 103 (repealed 1795).
7. Richard A. Boswell, "Racism and Immigration Law: Prospects for Reform after 9/11?," *Journal of Gender, Race and Justice* 7 (2003): 315, 317.
8. Act of Mar. 3, 1875, ch. 141, § 5, 18 Stat. 477 (repealed 1974).
9. Act of Aug. 3, 1882, ch. 376, § 2, 22 Stat. 214.
10. Kevin R. Johnson, *Opening the Floodgates: Why America Needs to Rethink Its Borders and Immigration Laws* (New York: New York University Press, 2007), 52.
11. Act of Feb. 5, 1917, ch. 29, § 3, 39 Stat. 875, 875–77 (repealed 1952). Under the act, "all aliens over sixteen years of age, physically capable of reading" must be able to do so or they would not be admitted into the United States. Furthermore, the act listed numerous offenses for which an alien could be deported and prohibited immigration from a broader portion of Asia.
12. The following works provide exhaustive examinations of this country's immigration history: Lawrence H. Fuchs, *The American Kaleidoscope: Race, Ethnicity, and the Civil Culture* (Hanover: Wesleyan University Press, 1990); John Higham, *Send These to Me: Immigrants in Urban America* (Baltimore: Johns Hopkins University Press, 1984); John Higham, *Strangers in the Land: Patterns of American Nativism, 1860–1925* (New Brunswick: Rutgers University Press, 1955); Bill Ong Hing, *Making and Remaking Asian America through Immigration Policy, 1850–1990* (Stanford: Stanford University Press, 1993); Mae M. Ngai, *Impossible Subjects: Illegal Aliens and the Making of Modern America* (Princeton: Princeton University Press, 2005); Kevin R. Johnson, *The Huddled Masses Myth: Immigration and Civil Rights* (Philadelphia: Temple University Press, 2004); and Gerald L. Neuman, *Strangers to the Constitution* (Princeton: Princeton University Press, 1996).
13. See, e.g., Johnson, *Opening the Floodgates*, 46.
14. Ibid., 80–81. The terms of the Migrant and Seasonal Agricultural Worker Protection Act identify the typical abuses against such workers, including unpaid wages and poor working conditions. Migrant and Seasonal Agricultural Worker

Protection Act, 29 U.S.C. §§ 1801-1872 (1994). Also see Johnson, "The Forgotten 'Repatriation,'" 4–5. This country's historical treatment of Latino and Latina workers from South and Central America reminds this author of the Clash song "Should I Stay or Should I Go," but instead of questioning whether anyone should stay or go, this country has repeatedly begged immigrant workers, "Please stay," only to scream shortly thereafter, "Now go!"

15. See Ronald Takaki, *Strangers from a Different Shore: A History of Asian Americans* (Boston: Little, Brown, 1989), 111, 116–17. Interestingly, the 1879 state constitution of California stated, "The presence of foreigners ineligible to become citizens of the United States is declared to be dangerous to the well-being of the state, and the legislature shall discourage their immigration by all the means within its power. Asiatic coolieism is a form of human slavery, and is forever prohibited in this state, and all contracts for coolie labor shall be void." Cal. Const., art. XIX, § 4 (repealed 1952).

16. Johnson, *The Huddled Masses Myth*, 17–18. See also Fong Yue Ting v. United States, 149 U.S. 698 (1893); Chae Chan Ping v. United States (Chinese Exclusion Case), 130 U.S. 581, 609 (1889). As I and other authors have noted, during the period of anti-Asian immigrant efforts, the U.S. Supreme Court decided the infamous Scott v. Sanford (Dred Scott), 60 U.S. 393 (1856), which similarly concluded that African Americans were excluded from eligibility for citizenship. See also Ediberto Román, "The Citizenship Dialectic," *Georgetown Immigration Law Journal* 20 (2006): 557, 576 (describing the Supreme Court's endorsement of "unequal treatment and inferior status of various groups that should have been considered citizens"). Also see Gabriel J. Chin, "Segregation's Last Stronghold: Race Discrimination and the Constitutional Law of Immigration," *UCLA Law Review* 46 (1998): 1, 14 n. 83. Immigration Act of 1924, ch. 190, § 11(d), 43 Stat. 153, 159 (repealed 1952). For numeric quotas established by the Immigration Act of 1924, see History Matters, "Who Was Shut Out? Immigration Quotas, 1925–1927," accessed Sept. 5, 2008, http:// historymatters.gmu.edu/d/5078.

17. See Johnson, *Opening the Floodgates*, 53.

18. U.S. Department of Health and Human Services, "Mental Health: Culture, Race, and Ethnicity—A Supplement to Mental Health: A Report of the Surgeon General," 2001, 41.

19. Johnson, *The Huddled Masses Myth*, 18. See also United States v. Thind, 261 U.S. 204, 214–15 (1923) ("As so understood and used, whatever may be the speculations of the ethnologist, [the words 'free white persons' do] not include the body of people to whom the appellee belongs"); and Ozawa v. United States, 260 U.S. 178, 198 (1922) ("The applicant, in the case now under consideration, however, is clearly of a race which is not Caucasian and therefore belongs entirely outside the zone on the negative side"). See generally Ian F. Haney Lopez, *White by Law: The Legal Construction of Race* (New York: New York University Press, 1997).

20. David J. Weber, ed., *Foreigners in Their Native Land: Historical Roots of the Mexican Americans* (Albuquerque: University of New Mexico Press, 1973, 2003); Andrés Reséndez, *Changing National Identities at the Frontier: Texas and New Mexico, 1800–1850* (New York: Cambridge University Press, 2004); Samuel Truett and Elliott Young, eds., *Continental Crossroads: Remapping US-Mexico Borderlands History* (Durham: Duke University Press, 2004); Rachel C. St. John, "Line in the Sand: The Desert Border between the United States and Mexico, 1848–1934" (PhD diss., Stanford University, 2005); Jeremy Adelman and Stephen Aron, "From Borderlands to Borders: Empires, Nation-States, and the Peoples in Between in North American History," *American Historical Review* 14 (1999): 814–41; Linda B. Hall and Don M. Coerver, *Revolution on the Border: The United States and Mexico, 1910–1920* (Albuquerque: University of New Mexico Press, 1988); Ramón Gutiérrez and Elliott Young, "Transnationalizing Borderlands History," *Western Historical Quarterly* 41 (2010): 27–53; Oscar J. Martínez, ed., *U.S.-Mexico Borderlands: Historical and Contemporary Perspectives* (Wilmington: Scholarly Resources, 1996).

21. Tom Head, "Why I Support Amnesty for Undocumented Immigrants," http://civilliberty.about.com/od/immigrantsrights/a/amnesty_3.htm.

22. See Ediberto Román, *Citizenship and Its Exclusions: A Classical, Constitutional, and Critical Race Critique* (New York: New York University Press, 2010), 133.

23. Mae M. Ngai, "The Strange Career of the Illegal Alien: Immigration Restriction and Deportation Policy in the United States, 1921–1965," *Law and History Review* 21 (2003): 69, 75–76. It should be noted that data on apprehensions and deportations do not represent all unlawful entries and are further skewed by policy decisions to police certain areas or populations and not others. On methodologies employed, see "Illegal Alien Resident Population," *INS Statistical Yearbook* (1998); see also Barry Edmonston, Jeffrey Passel, and Frank Bean, *Undocumented Migration to the United States: IRCA and the Experience of the 1980s* (Santa Monica: Rand, 1990), 16–18, 27.

24. Head, "Why I Support Amnesty."

25. Alexandra Villarreal O'Rourke, Comment, "Embracing Reality: The Guest Worker Program Revisited," *Harvard Latino Law Review* 9 (2006): 179, 180.

26. David G. Gutiérrez, *Walls and Mirrors: Mexican Americans, Mexican Immigrants, and the Politics of Ethnicity* (Berkeley: University of California Press, 1995), 45.

27. Román, *Citizenship and Its Exclusions*, 133.

28. Desmond King, *Making Americans: Immigration, Race, and the Origins of the Diverse Democracy* (Cambridge: Harvard University Press, 2000), 231.

29. Lisa A. Flores, "Constructing Rhetorical Borders: Peons, Illegal Aliens, and Competing Narratives of Immigration," *Critical Studies in Media Communication* 20 (2003): 362.

30. See Villarreal O'Rourke, "Embracing Reality"; and Kiera LoBreglio, Note, "The Border Security and Immigration Improvement Act: A Modern Solution to a Historic Problem," *St. John's Law Review* 78 (2004): 933, 936.
31. Flores, "Constructing Rhetorical Borders," 375.
32. See ibid.; and Ngai, "The Strange Career of the Illegal Alien."
33. Flores, "Constructing Rhetorical Borders," 376.
34. Council on Foreign Relations, "U.S.–Mexico Timeline," http://www.cfr.org/interactives/Timeline_Mexico/timeline-wrapper.swf?156548762.
35. See Johnson, "The Forgotten 'Repatriation'"; and Francisco E. Balderrama and Raymond Rodríguez, *Decade of Betrayal: Mexican Repatriation in the 1930s* (Albuquerque: University of New Mexico Press, 1995), 98–99.
36. Johnson, "The Forgotten 'Repatriation,'" 4.
37. Council on Foreign Relations, "U.S.–Mexico Timeline."
38. Johnson, "The Forgotten 'Repatriation,'" 9–10.
39. Román, *Citizenship and Its Exclusions*, 134. See also Villarreal O'Rourke, "Embracing Reality"; Lorenzo A. Alvarado, Comment, "A Lesson from My Grandfather, the Bracero," *Chicano-Latino Law Review* 22 (2001): 55; and Kitty Calavita, *Inside the State: The Bracero Program, Immigration, and the I.N.S.* (New York: Routledge, 1992), 19.
40. Román, *Citizenship and Its Exclusions*, 135.
41. Ngai, *Impossible Subjects*, 139.
42. LoBreglio, "The Border Security and Immigration Improvement Act," 937. See also Kristi Morgan, "Evaluating Guest Worker Programs in the U.S.: A Comparison of the Bracero Program and President Bush's Proposed Immigration Reform Plan," *Berkeley La Raza Law Journal* 15 (2004): 125; Maria Möller, "Philadelphia's Mexican War Workers," *Pennsylvania Legacies* 3, no. 2 (November 2003): 16; and Julian Samora and Patricia Vandel Simon, *A History of the Mexican American People* (Notre Dame: University of Notre Dame Press, 1977), 136–37.
43. Román, *Citizenship and Its Exclusions*, 135. See also LoBreglio, "The Border Security and Immigration Improvement Act," 937; and Barbara A. Driscoll, *The Tracks North: The Railroad Bracero Program of World War II* (Austin: Center for Mexican American Studies, 1999), 56.
44. Ngai, *Impossible Subjects*, 143.
45. Román, *Citizenship and Its Exclusions*, 135. See also Driscoll, *Tracks North*, 56.
46. Román, *Citizenship and Its Exclusions*, 136. See also Juan Ramón García, *Operation Wetback: The Mass Deportation of Mexican American Undocumented Workers in 1954* (New York: Praeger, 1980), 40, 169, 230–31; Samora and Vandel Simon, *History of the Mexican American People*, 136; Calavita, *Inside the State*, 49–50, 53–54, 142. Ultimately, the United States allowed roughly five million Mexicans to enter and work in the United States as Braceros under the program, which ended in 1965.
47. Ngai, *Impossible Subjects*, 149.

48. Samora and Vandel Simon, *History of the Mexican American People*, 136.
49. See, e.g., Julian Samora, *Los Mojados: The Wetback Story* (Notre Dame: University of Notre Dame Press, 1971), 75–77.
50. See García, *Operation Wetback*, 227–29.
51. Ibid., 227–30.
52. Steven Bender, *Running for the Border* (New York: New York University Press, 2011), 14–15.
53. Ibid., 13.
54. Flores, "Constructing Rhetorical Borders," 370.
55. Ibid., 374.
56. Ibid., 376.
57. Ngai, *Impossible Subjects*, 8.
58. See Román, *Citizenship and Its Exclusions*, 137, for detailed discussion of the laws passed by the 109th Congress.

NOTES TO CHAPTER 6

1. Judd Legum, "Breaking News: Rush Limbaugh Syndicator Suspends Advertising for Two Weeks," Think Progress, March 12, 2012, http://thinkprogress.org/media/2012/03/12/443195/breaking-rush-limbaugh-syndicator-suspends-national-ads-for-two-weeks/?mobile=nc.
2. Sheila T. Murphy, "The Impact of Factual versus Fictional Media Portrayals on Cultural Stereotypes," *Annals of the American Academy of Political and Social Science* 560 (1998): 166.
3. American Values Institute, "What Is Implicit Bias?," http://americansforamericanvalues.org/unconsciousbias/.
4. Jerry Kang, "Implicit Bias: A Primer for Courts," Prepared for the National Campaign to Ensure the Racial and Ethnic Fairness of America's State Courts, August 2009, 1–2, available at http://www.scribd.com/doc/45313723/Implicit-Bias-A-Primer-for-Courts-Kang.
5. Erving Goffman, *Stigma: Notes on the Management of Spoiled Identity* (1963; New York: Simon and Schuster, 1986), 2.
6. Roger E. Kasperson and Jeanne Kasperson, *Social Contours of Risk*, vol. 1, *Publics, Risk Communication and the Social* (New York: Routledge, 2005), 166.
7. Paul Rozin, "Technological Stigma: Some Perspectives from the Study of Contagion," in *Risk, Media, and Stigma: Understanding Public Challenges to Modern Science and Technology*, ed. James Flynn, Paul Slovic, and Howard Kunreuther (New York: Routledge, 2001), 33.
8. Howard Kunreuther and Paul Slovic, "Coping with Stigma: Challenges and Opportunities," in Flynn et al., eds., *Risk, Media, and Stigma*.
9. Ibid., 335.
10. U.S. Commission on Civil Rights, *Window Dressing on the Set: Women and Minorities in Television*, August 1977.

11. Ibid.
12. Minnesota Advisory Committee to the U.S. Commission on Civil Rights, "Stereo-typing of Minorities by the News Media in Minnesota," May 1993, 35, http://www.law.umaryland.edu/marshall/usccr/documents/cr12st42z.pdf.
13. Margaret M. Russell, "Race and the Dominant Gaze: Narratives of Law and Inequality in Popular Film," *Legal Studies Forum* 15 (1991): 244.
14. Gregory R. Maio, Victoria M. Esses, and David W. Bell, "The Formation of Atti-tudes toward New Immigrant Groups," *Journal of Applied Social Psychology* 24 (1994): 1764–65, http://psych.cf.ac.uk/home2/maio/Maio%20et%20al%20JASP%20 1994.pdf.
15. Gregory R. Maio, David W. Bell, and Victoria M. Esses, "Ambivalence and Persua-sion: The Processing of Messages about Immigrant Groups," *Journal of Experi-mental Social Psychology* 32 (1996): 513–14, http://psych.cf.ac.uk/home2/maio/ Maio%20et%20al%20JESP%201996.pdf.
16. Ediberto Román, "Who Exactly Is Living La Vida Loca? The Legal and Political Consequences of Latino-Latina Ethnic and Racial Stereotypes in Film and Other Media," *Journal of Gender, Race and Justice* 4 (2000): 37, 42–48.
17. Andres Oppenheimer, "Time to Hit Back against Anti-Latino Bigotry," *Miami Herald*, July 22, 2007, A14. See also, e.g., Tom I. Romero II, "¿La Raza Latina? Mul-tiracial Ambivalence, Color Denial, and the Emergence of a Tri-Ethnic Jurispru-dence at the End of the Twentieth Century," *New Mexico Law Review* 37 (2007): 245, 306, n. 406.
18. Kevin Johnson, "Race, the Immigration Laws, and Domestic Race Relations: A 'Magic Mirror' into the Heart of Darkness," *Indiana Law Journal* 73 (1998).
19. Ibid., 1155.
20. Ibid., 1132.

NOTES TO CHAPTER 7
1. See generally Bill Ong Hing, "Beyond the Rhetoric of Assimilation and Cultural Pluralism: Addressing the Tension of Separatism and Conflict in an Immigration-Driven Multicultural Society," *California Law Review* 81 (1993): 863 (examining the race- and culture-based rationales of modern assimilationist sentiments regarding immigration).
2. Fred Barnes, "Immigration Overkill?," *Weekly Standard*, Aug. 18, 2007.
3. See Kevin R. Johnson, "September 11 and Mexican Immigrants: Collateral Dam-age Comes Home," *DePaul Law Review* 52 (2003): 849, 852–53, 859–60.
4. See Michael Gerson, "Erasing America? Latinos Don't Endanger the Nation, Just Republicans Who Don't Get It," *Pittsburgh Post-Gazette*, May 25, 2007, B7.
5. George W. Bush, State of the Union Address, Jan. 28, 2008, transcript available at http:// www.whitehouse.gov/news/releases/2008/01/20080128-13.html.
6. David Olinger, "Border Wars Personal Out West," *Denver Post*, Jan. 27, 2008, A16.
7. Ibid.

8. According to Jeb Bush, "new Americans strengthen our economy. We need more people to come to this country, ready to work and to contribute their creativity to our economy. U.S. immigration policies should reflect that principle. Just as Republicans believe in free trade of goods, we should support the freer flow of human talent." Quoted in Maggie Haberman, "Jeb Bush Warns GOP about Losing Hispanic Voters," Politico, Jan., 25, 2012, http://www.politico.com/blogs/burns-haberman/2012/01/jeb-bush-cautions-the-gop-about-losing-hispanic-voters-112340.html.

9. Senator Marco Rubio's remarks at the 2012 Hispanic Leadership Network conference, Jan. 27, 2012, http://www.c-spanvideo.org/program/303952-2.

10. Comments by President Obama on Deferred Action for Childhood Arrivals, June 15, 2012, http://www.uscrirefugees.org/2010Website/5_Resources/5_4_For_Lawyers/5_4_6_DREAM/Transcript_President'_DREAM_Act_Remarks.pdf.

11. Michael Gerson, "The Right Ought to Embrace Hispanics, Not Fear Them," *Newark Star-Ledger*, May 29, 2007, 11. See generally Derrick Bell Jr., "*Brown v. Board of Education* and the Interest-Convergence Dilemma," *Harvard Law Review* 93 (1980): 518.

12. U.S. Census Bureau, "State and County Quick Facts," http://quickfacts.census.gov/qfd/states/00000.html.

13. Paul Taylor et al., "An Awakened Giant: The Hispanic Electorate Is Likely to Double by 2030," Pew Hispanic Center, Nov. 14, 2012, http://www.pewhispanic.org/2012/11/14/an-awakened-giant-the-hispanic-electorate-is-likely-to-double-by-2030/.

14. See "Latinos and the 2006 Mid-Term Election," Fact Sheet, Pew Hispanic Center, Nov. 27, 2006, http://pewhispanic.org/files/factsheets/26.pdf.

15. See, e.g., Victor C. Romero, "On Elián and the Aliens: A Political Solution to the Plenary Power Problem," *New York University Journal of Legislation and Public Policy* 4 (2000–2001): 343, 367–68.

16. See generally Ruth Morris and Elizabeth Baier, "Hispanic Voters Could Make GOP Pay for Defeat of Immigration Legislation," *South Florida Sun-Sentinel*, July 1, 2007.

17. Mort Kondracke, "Immigration Failure Gives Senate Profile in Political Cowardice," Real Clear Politics, July 2, 2007, http://www.realclearpolitics.com/articles/2007/07/immigration_failure_profile_in.html.

18. Olinger, "Border Wars Personal Out West."

19. Mark Hugo Lopez and Paul Taylor, "Latino Voters in the 2012 Election," Pew Hispanic Center, Nov. 7, 2012, http://www.pewhispanic.org/2012/11/07/latino-voters-in-the-2012-election/.

20. David Lightman, "Democrats Sidestep Immigration Issue," *Miami Herald*, Nov. 15, 2007, A6.

21. Barnes, "Immigration Overkill?"

22. Matt Barreto, "New Poll: Immigration Policy Stance Directly Tied to Winning the Latino Vote," Latino Decisions, March

5, 2013, http://www.latinodecisions.com/blog/2013/03/05/
new-poll-immigration-policy-stance-directly-tied-to-winning-the-latino-vote/.

23. Andres Oppenheimer, "Time to Hit Back against Anti-Latino Bigotry," *Miami Herald*, July 22, 2007, A14. "Ya Basta" could be translated as "Enough Already."

24. Barreto, "New Poll."

25. Edward Telles, "Mexican Americans and the American Nation: A Response to Professor Huntington," *Aztlán*, Fall 2006, 7, 22.

26. See Lani Guinier and Gerald Torres, *The Miner's Canary: Enlisting Race, Resisting Power, Transforming Democracy* (Cambridge: Harvard University Press, 2002), 9–10 (advocating that individuals identify themselves with political parties, rather than racial or social classifications).

27. See Ediberto Román, "Coalitions and Collective Memories: A Search for Common Ground," *Mercer Law Review* 58 (2007): 637, 643–44; Sameer M. Ashar, "Immigration Enforcement and Subordination: The Consequences of Racial Profiling after September 11," *Connecticut Law Review* 34 (2002): 1185, 1199; and Bill Ong Hing, "Vigilante Racism: The De-Americanization of Immigrant America," *Michigan Journal of Race and Law* 7 (2002): 441, 456.

28. See Román, "Coalitions and Collective Memories," 643–44.

29. "Jim Gilchrist of Minuteman Project on Immigration, Terror, Elections," Global Politician, May 31, 2007, available at http://immigration.procon.org/view.answers.php?questionID=000774.

30. Ediberto Román and Christopher B. Carbot, "Freeriders and Diversity in the Legal Academy: A New Dirty Dozen List?" *Indiana Law Journal* 83, no. 4 (October 2008).

31. Rajeev Goyle and David Jaeger, "Deporting the Undocumented: A Cost Assessment," Center for American Progress, July 2005, http://www.americanprogress.org/issues/immigration/report/2005/07/26/1581/deporting-the-undocumented-a-cost-assessment/.

32. "It Isn't Amnesty," editorial, *New York Times*, March 29, 2006.

33. Tom Ridge, "Immigration and Security," *Washington Times*, Sept. 10, 2006.

34. "McCain Statement on Border Security and Immigration Reform Legislation," March 30, 2006, http://www.mccain.senate.gov/public/index.cfm?FuseAction=PressOffice.Speeches&ContentRecord_id=ce7596a1-0670-40f0-b054-e5c3650c02dd&Region_id=&Issue_id=.

35. New Sanctuary Movement, "Pledge and Covenant," available at www.uua.org/documents/washingtonoffice/sanctuary_issuebrief.pdf.

36. Indy Bay, "Conference Call for Child Citizen Protection Act," Feb. 28, 2007, http://www.indybay.org/newsitems/2007/02/22/18367305.php.

37. Families for Freedom, "Deportation 101: From Raids to Deportation," June 26, 2007, www.familiesforfreedom.org.

38. American Friends Service Committee, "'Legalization' or 'Amnesty'? Understanding the Debate," http://www.afsc.org/, also at http://immigration.procon.org/view.answers.php?questionID=000770.

39. Quotes from Neugebauer, Sensenbrenner, Tancredo, and Paul available at http://immigration.procon.org/view.answers. php?questionID=000771#answer-id-003799.

40. John Kerry, statement in Democratic primary debate, Sept. 4, 2003, available at http://immigration.procon.org/view.answers. php?questionID=000771#answer-id-003799.

41. John J. Sweeney, "Letter to the National and International Union Presidents," June 1, 2005, available at http://immigration.procon.org/view.answers. php?questionID=001362#answer-id-008315.

42. "Fact Sheet: Fair and Secure Immigration Reform," White House press release, Jan. 7, 2004; see also, e.g., "Bush Reiterates Call for Guest Worker Program," March 23, 2006, http://www.america.gov/st/washfile-english/2006/March/200603 23124207ASrelliM0.4169123.html.

43. "President Bush Proposes New Temporary Worker Program," Jan. 7, 2004, http:// georgewbush-whitehouse.archives.gov/news/releases/2004/01/20040107-3.html.

44. Bill Ong Hing, *Deporting Our Souls: Values, Morality, and Immigration Policy* (New York: New York University Press, 2009), 39, 41–42.

45. The Secure Borders, Economic Opportunity and Immigration Reform Act of 2007 (S. 1348), also known as the Comprehensive Immigration Reform Act of 2007.

46. "Gang of Eight, Obama Present Immigration Reform Proposals in Washington," Hanlon Law Group, http://www.visaandgreencard.com/CM/Articles/Gang-of-eight-Obama-present-immigration-reform-proposals-in-Washington.asp. See also Emily Deruy, "Gang of Eight Accelerates Immigration Reform Pace," ABC News/Univision, Jan. 30, 2013, http://abcnews.go.com/ABC_Univision/Politics/gang-accelerates-immigration-reform-pace/story?id=18354593.

47. "Remarks by the President on Comprehensive Immigration Reform," White House press release, Jan. 29, 2013, http://www.whitehouse.gov/the-press-office/2013/01/29/remarks-president-comprehensive-immigration-reform. See also Napp Nazworth, "Obama Lends Support to 'Gang of Eight' Immigration Reform Plan," Christian Post, Jan. 30, 2013, http://www.christianpost.com/news/obama-lends-support-to-gang-of-eight-immigration-reform-plan-89107/.

Pew Hispanic Center, 48–50, 80, 88–89, 137
Population. *See* Empirical data on immigration

Race-based immigration quotas, 3
Rhetorical devices, 17–18, 25, 26, 27. *See also* Entertainers against immigrants; Media hatemongering
Richards, Michael, 27. *See also* Entertainers against immigrants
Romney, Mitt, 20, 135, 137; attack on Rick Perry, 21–23; "self-deportation," 22; debate with Rudy Giuliani, 23
Rubio, Marco, 136

Salazar, Ken, 21–22
"Self-deportation," 22, 135. *See also* Rhetorical devices; Romney, Mitt
September 11, 2001, 2
Somos Republicans, 20; letter to Herman Cain, 20. *See also* Cain, Herman
Spencer, Glenn, 33. See also Extremist vigilante organizations; New nativists
Stigma: immigrant, 127–28, 132; foreign, 132; media influence and, 128–29; public policy and, 132

Tancredo, Tom, 24, 133, 144. *See also* Media hatemongering; Violence against immigrants

Transference and displacement, 130–31; psychological theory, 131
TSA profiling, 35. *See also* Violence against immigrants

Undocumented immigrants, 5–7; attacks by politicians, 7; on cultural stigma, 9, 11, 14–15, 17; on the economy, 21; on media attacks, 7. *See also* Media hatemongering; Stigma, immigrant; Tancredo, Tom

Violence against immigrants, 34; anti-Hispanic hate crime (2003–2007), 40; Jeffrey Conroy, 35; Raul Flores murders, 37; San Francisco violence, 37; TSA profiling, 35; Luis Eduardo Ramirez Zavala, 37
Voter alienation, 138

Wages, domestic, impact of immigration on, 73; National Bureau of Economic Research working paper (2008), 74–75; President's Council of Economic Advisors report (2007), 76; survey of economist David Card, 77–78; "Task Specialization, Immigration, and Wages" report (2008), 76
War of the Worlds, 2, 133
Williams, Kat, 25. *See also* Entertainers against immigrants

Ediberto Román is a nationally acclaimed scholar and an award-winning educator with broad teaching interests and an extensive scholarship portfolio. A prolific scholar, he has published numerous legal articles, essays, and book chapters on international law, securities regulation, evidence, constitutional law, critical race theory, postcolonial discourse, and law and literature. These articles have appeared in the leading law journals of Harvard, UC Berkeley, Georgetown, Indiana, Houston, UC Davis, Iowa, Miami, Villanova, San Diego, Rutgers, Florida, and Florida State and have been widely cited for their unique contributions to legal theory. His first two books on colonialism, citizenship, and nationality—*The Other American Colonies: An International and Constitutional Law Examination of the United States' Nineteenth and Twentieth Century Island Conquests* (Carolina Academic Press) and *Citizenship and Its Exclusions: A Classical, Constitutional, and Critical Race Critique* (New York University Press)—have received critical acclaim. His more recent books are *Those Damned Immigrants: America's Hysteria over Undocumented Immigration* (New York University Press) and *Understanding Immigration* (Carolina Academic Press). His scholarly productivity and national reputation have led him to recently be named series editor for the New York University Press series "Citizenship and Migration in the Americas." In just over a year since its creation, the series is scheduled to publish books from many of the academy's leading immigration and constitutional law scholars. In addition, Román is a frequent commentator on numerous blogs, such as the Faculty Lounge. He is the founder of the Nuestras Voces Latinas Blog and is a regular columnist for the *Huffington Post*.

Román also spends considerable time advocating for undocumented student rights. In that capacity, he has advised numerous interested parties, including student groups, members of the media, and politicians on matters such as the DREAM Act and anti-immigrant state legislation. A sought-after speaker and public intellectual, he is frequently asked to appear on Spanish- and English-language television and radio by local, national, and international media to provide his views on constitutional law and immigration policy. When not engaged in the above, he keeps himself busy being a proud father of five and a practitioner of tae kwon do.